Victorian Word-Painting and Narrative
Toward the Blending of Genres

Nineteenth-Century Studies

Juliet McMaster, Series Editor

University Professor
University of Alberta

Other Titles in This Series

Victorian Word-Painting and Narrative
Toward the Blending of Genres

by
Rhoda L. Flaxman

UMI Research
Press

Ann Arbor, Michigan

Produced and distributed by
UMI Research Press
an imprint of
University Microfilms, Inc.
Ann Arbor, Michigan 48106

Library of Congress Cataloging in Publication Data

Flaxman, Rhoda L. (Rhoda Leven), 1940-
Victorian word-painting and narrative.

(Nineteenth-century studies)
Revision of thesis (Ph.D.)—Brown University, 1982.
Bibliography: p.
Includes index.
 1. English literature—19th century—History and
criticism. 2. Picturesque, The, in literature.
3. Description (Rhetoric) 4. Narration (Rhetoric)
5. Literary form. 6. Art and literature—Great Britain—
History—19th century. I. Title. II. Series:
Nineteenth-century studies (Ann Arbor, Mich.)
PR468.P53F5 1987   820'.9'008   86-30753
ISBN 0-8357-1787-9 (alk. paper)

To Pauline and Irving Leven,
Allen,
Lisa, Cindy, David, and Jessica,
who in the narrative of my life
paint the colors of fulfillment

and

to Joan, my sister,

Love,

Rhoda

4/30/87

Contents

Acknowledgments

Though fascination with interconnections between art and literature has formed a steady subtext to my teaching and learning since my undergraduate days at Bryn Mawr College, ideas for this particular book really took shape over the last several years while I was at Brown University and Wheaton College. During this time I was most influenced by and owe the greatest debt to Professor George P. Landow of Brown. He first encouraged me as teacher and mentor, and continues to do so now as colleague and friend. I'd like to thank him publicly for his guidance and support.

I'd also like to thank Professors Roger B. Henkle of Brown and Barbara Kiefer Lewalski of Harvard for reading the first version of this study and offering valuable suggestions.

To Mary Patterson McPherson, President of Bryn Mawr College, I would like to express my admiration for the example she consistently sets for me of what is possible for women to achieve and the graceful style in which to achieve it.

Lastly, I want to inscribe the name of Anita Glass in my book, and to express my wish that she were here to share my pleasure in its publication.

Introduction: Victorian Word-Painting

This study establishes the distinctive features of Victorian word-painting in the works of Charles Dickens and Alfred, Lord Tennyson and suggests ways in which word-painting contributes both to the attrition of narrative and to the development of fused modes previously generic to prose and poetry in some "hybrid" works of Modernist and post-Modernist literature. Word-painting is a term used here to refer to extended passages of visually oriented description that are composed with attention to framing devices, recurrent iconographic and formal motifs, and a carefully established, consistent perspective. I utilize a broadly historical and descriptive approach, adapting aesthetic categories from Erwin Panofsky's *Studies in Iconology* to a generally semiotic methodology.[1] An iconographic analysis of word-painting approaches the functioning of verbal visualizations as a system of signs. As such, they can be described according to Panofsky's scheme, which divides the analysis of works of art into preiconographical description, iconographical analysis, and iconological interpretation.

My interest in the relationship between word-painting and narrative emerges from a concern with formal parallels between the visual arts and literature of the Victorian period. Word-painting, which often appears to move verbal art into the realm of the spatial rather than the temporal, may be one element that blurs Lessing's famous distinction between poetry as exclusively a temporal and kinetic art, and painting as exclusively a spatial and static one.[2]

A study of word-painting in relation to narrative is justified on several counts. First, no one has suggested the outlines of a tradition of word-painting in the Victorian period, though this feature contributes significantly to the evolution of "hybrid" works popular toward the end of the nineteenth century.[3] Secondly, few have examined this feature through close readings of specific passages from key texts in the period. Recently, critics such as Miller, Hardy, Landow, Priestley, Bloom, Shaw, Joseph, Sinfield, and others have begun to examine formal elements in Victorian literature and to connect them to philosophical concerns of the age.[4] But, thus far, no one has attempted to sketch the tradition after 1800, nor to consider the relationship between word-painting and changing forms of narrative poetry and fiction.

The nineteenth century in England indisputably saw the ascendancy of the novel as the dominant literary art form. While the emphasis in the early English novel had been upon the creation of an extended prose narrative—a lively story unfolding temporally—nonnarrative writing, occasionally presented as word-painting, remained a strong "secondary" strain in the novel. The integration of "mood" writing from the romance and Gothic strains into the primarily realistic tradition of the novel might be expected to change both content and form of the work in which it is embedded.

Close readings of specific prose passages from texts by Radcliffe, Scott, Dickens, and Virginia Woolf suggest the way in which word-paintings, beginning in the Gothic novel as an interruption in narrative flow, gradually invade story, become inseparable from it, and, in some cases, take over narrative completely. Along with Hardy, Conrad, Lawrence, and Joyce, Woolf's experimental blendings of lyric and narrative help to establish a new direction and form for the nonrealistic strain which flowers in post-Modernist works by Robbe-Grillet, Pynchon, Barth, Coover, and many others.

Extended passages of primarily visually oriented description force a different time structure on the novel when they stop the story for a moment, or "freeze" time, in order to fill in setting or to provide atmosphere for the story. My study will suggest that word-paintings serving more complicated functions in the works of Dickens and Tennyson will gradually supplant the relatively simple uses for word-paintings in the early novel and lyric poetry. In addition, the development of word-painting in Dickens and Tennyson assumes an almost identical pattern.

This study of Victorian word-painting begins with a brief examination of Radcliffe's word-painting because she is one of the first novelists to elevate visually oriented descriptions to a prominent position in English fiction. It ends with a discussion of Virginia Woolf's "prosepoem," *The Waves*. A comparison between the word-paintings of these two writers indicates the degree to which writers continually struggle to work out the tensions between narration and description. Although Radcliffe and Woolf are widely separated both by time and by enormous thematic and stylistic differences, they resolve the relationship between word-painting and narration in strikingly similar ways in *The Mysteries of Udolpho* and *The Waves*.

Between these writers, one finds other important writers beginning to play with point of view and with both kinetic and static narrations of landscape. Ruskin, for example, attempts more elaborate schemata for word-paintings than had been tried previously, using them to underscore a theme or moral lesson. Ruskin may have been the first to use the phrase "word-painting," but since most of his extended visually oriented descriptions occur in essays rather than novels or poetry, his word-paintings will not concern me here. Instead, after a brief look at Scott's word-paintings, the first section of the present study focuses on representative descriptive passages from an early, middle and late novel by Charles Dickens in order to demonstrate the general movement from simple to more complex uses of word-paintings and their increasingly well-exe-cuted integration with narrative. In *Barnaby Rudge,* for example, the pictur-esque determines the view of landscape, but more complex uses of word-paint-ings evolve in *David Copperfield* and *Little Dorrit. David Copperfield* is an especially interesting transitional work in which Dickens reserves the pictur-esque point of view for David's childhood memories and moves on to word-portraits and verbal tableaux to express a more problematical relationship be-tween the protagonist and the phenomenological world he perceives. And in a late novel, *Little Dorrit,* Dickens fuses description with narration by utilizing the visual as symbolic subtext to narration.

Passages of extended visually oriented description, closer to traditional concerns of lyric poetry than to the narrative emphasis of the novel, seem to draw the forms of novels and poems closer together toward the end of the nineteenth century. A discussion of the development of Victorian word-painting in the poetic tradition begins with a brief examination of representative pass-ages from James Thomson and William Wordsworth. Thomson serves as in-novative word-painter in poetry much as Radcliffe serves that function in the novel. Thomson's word-paintings in *The Seasons* offer a repertory of percep-tions and effects on which later poets draw. Later, during the Romantic period, Wordsworth and Coleridge signal increasing interest in narrative verse as rigid formal rules for poetry progressively loosen. Passages from Wordsworth's "Tintern Abbey" and *The Prelude* stand here for interesting relationships be-tween narrative and descriptive materials in early nineteenth-century poetry.

Word-painting, of course, reflects a poet's attitude toward nature, and the line from Thomson through Wordsworth to Tennyson and T. S. Eliot affirms the growing fragmentation both of the relationship between man and nature and the expression of this shattering relationship in new poetic forms. The attendant problem of fusing a segmented structure into a long narrative poet concerns Tennyson in *The Princess, In Memoriam,* and *Idylls of the King* as much as it concerns Eliot in *The Waste Land.*

Just as Dickens's novels provide fertile ground for exploring the relation-ship between word-painting and narrative in the novel tradition, so Tennyson's poetry is pivotal to a discussion of new strategies for poetry in the Victorian period. Like Dickens, Tennyson's word-paintings move from simple to more complex uses as his career progresses. The stages of this development are strik-ingly similar in the writings of these two major Victorian figures, evolving from heavy dependence on an eighteenth-century visual aesthetic toward the use of verbal tableaux and, finally, to symbolic correlatives for narrative ac-tions and states of consciousness.

In important long poems such as *The Princess, In Memoriam,* and *Idylls of the King*, Tennyson experiments with a confluence of narrative, descriptive, and lyrical modes. *Idylls of the King,* which emphasizes narrative most strongly of all Tennyson's works, recapitulates Tennyson's kinds and uses of word-paintings in a pattern significant to its narrative structure. The problem of coherence that Tennyson faces in his major long poems proves instructive to poets like Eliot and Pound who come after him. In contrast to writers interested in clear narrative line and temporal verisimilitude, Tennyson often is best at lovingly detailed descriptions of a moment of "stopped time" where he frames and explores a single scene that opens up other "worlds" to the reader. The structure of fragments that results from such creative inclinations gives rise to a specific structural technique that begins to change the shape of poetry. In the hands of a Modernist like T. S. Eliot, the segmented panel structures of Tennyson, worked out fully, become the compositional technique of *The Waste Land*, "fragments . . . shored against . . . ruin."

A brief examination of Woolf's *The Waves* and Eliot's *The Waste Land* concludes the present study, suggesting ways in which word-painting contributes to a blending of the genres of fiction and poetry in later experimental works. The discussion speculates that word-painting has an important effect on the subversion of narrative, moving both genres toward a more discontinuous or, if you will, a more "poetic" structure in some post-Victorian works. In the poetic as well as the fictional tradition, a concern with the proper balance between narration and description continues to evolve to the present day.

A Note on Method

Groundwork for a study of Victorian word-painting has been laid by such critics as Male, Praz, Lee, and Hagstrum, but their interests are historical and cultural, rather than formal.[5] Other critics like Frank, Sypher, Uspensky, and Schapiro attempt to equate the formal concerns of the visual arts with suggestively similar elements of verbal style, but their conclusions are incomplete.[6] No one has yet formulated a terminology neutral enough to apply equally well to the visual and the verbal arts, although recent work in semiotics seems to offer hope for eventual formulations of this nature.[7] In the meantime, interarts critics would do well to heed the suggestion of Wellek and Warren that the various arts are best seen as a series of "dialectical relationships" rather than parallel or evolutionary phenomena.[8]

Instead of presenting a study of the "Zeitgeist," therefore, I will use a generally semiotic approach to establish the distinctive features of Victorian word-painting. By this I mean that the functioning of verbal visualizations will be approached as a system of signs not unlike the study of both the iconography (the subject matter or meaning) and the formal (or stylistic) properties in visual art. Such a study ought to lay bare both the pictorial and the symbolic equivalences of verbal art. Erwin Panofsky's work offers the most complete system for illuminating both aspects of art. Panofsky suggests a justification for adapting his methodology to the analysis of verbal, as well as visual art, in the following statement: "It is in the search for intrinsic meanings or content that the various humanistic disciplines meet on a common plane instead of serving as hand-maidens to each other" (p. 30). An amendment of Panofsky's method for the analysis of formal properties of verbal description might read: the various humanistic disciplines might enter into a dialogue about equally vivid manifestations of similar ideas in a study of their form.

Panofsky's system distinguishes three major areas of analysis, which suggests a useful structure for the study of verbal visualizations. In the present study, preiconographical description refers to the analysis of compositional methods of particular word-paintings that attempts to construct a paradigm for the ways different writers build their word-paintings. A formal analysis of stylistic characteristics notes the use of framing devices for the scene, the frequency and recurrence of iconographic elements or motifs, the rules of their composition, the use of color or of light and darkness, and the point of view (real or implied).

Panofsky's second level is iconographical analysis. By this he means the relating of artistic motifs and compositions to the themes or concepts which they represent or in which they participate. Whereas the preiconographical level involves the identification of form as pure form, the iconographical level links these forms with their "secondary or conventional" meanings.

The third level of Panofsky's scheme attempts to relate stylistic characteristics to trends of depicting visually oriented verbalizations in Victorian literature. Here, the utmost tact is required, for one wishes, not to erect a rigid system of meaning, but, rather, to remember that the components of any art constitute a language, and, as language, carry an arbitrary and conventional meaning, not one that is "inherent" or "natural." Often, meaning evolves from a series of oppositions in a given verbal or visual work; for example, a scene's drama is heightened by the contrast between darkness and light, or between enclosure and expansiveness. One must remember continually to aim for flexibility in the interpretation of verbal visualizations. For, in the last analysis, attempts to compare art and literature may be metaphorical rather than scientific.

Panofsky's first two levels of analysis offer the literary critic a useful methodology. His third level, which he calls iconological interpretation, takes us away from stylistic or formal considerations and into the area of social and cultural ones. This subject relates art to "those underlying principles which reveal the basic attitude of a nation, a period, a class, a religious or philosophical persuasion—unconsciously qualified by one personality and condensed into one work" (p. 7). The relationship of artistic motifs to their deeper social and cultural significance, while fascinating, lies beyond the scope of the present study.

Part One

Word-Painting and Narrative in the Novel

1

Preview: Word-Painting in Radcliffe and Scott

It is a truth nearly universally acknowledged by nineteenth-century critics that the eighteenth century lacks "eye." Critics like Harold Bloom and Carol Christ credit Victorian literature with a revolutionary advance in the fusion of the scientific and the poetic to record an emotionally charged natural world. Think, for instance, of Tennyson's "Mariana" or Rossetti's "The Woodspurge," where a hyperrealism infuses precise natural details with the spillover of feeling from observer to observed.

But has eighteenth-century writing been unjustly accused of lacking an adequate record of carefully observed visual detail? Further, may critics have overlooked the invention of a new method of description in the eighteenth century that begins to influence the form of the novel and the blending of genres of poetry and fiction?

This new method of description (which, borrowing from John Ruskin, I call word-painting) forms an important innovative feature in the work of eighteenth-century writers James Thomson and Ann Radcliffe, and compares interestingly with later word-paintings of Wordsworth, Scott, Dickens, and Tennyson. I begin this study by comparing two pre-Victorian novelists (Radcliffe and Scott) in order to define the feature, sketch the transitional moment between centuries as word-painting begins to evolve, and suggest some directions for the later history of word-painting in its relationship to narrative. Divided by genre, the second half of my study sets forth Thomson and Wordsworth as poetic precursors to Victorian word-painting.

First, what exactly is word-painting? This term refers to extended passages of visually oriented descriptions whose techniques emulate pictorial methods. Word-painters typically employ framing devices, recurrent iconographic motifs, careful compositional structures, and pay close attention to contrasts of light and dark, of color, volume, and mass. But the primary feature that distinguishes a genuine word-painting from a static catalogue of visual data is faithfulness to a precise and consistent perspective focused through the viewpoint of a particular spectator. This point of view often yields an effect we moderns call cinematic, implying progress from one element to the next in a "narrative of landscape." This narrative of landscape transforms a static catalogue of visual data into the dramatization of the visual. Word-painting, then, implying spatial progression through a landscape, offers a correlative to narrative. Increasingly, as one follows a chronological tradition of word-painting, one traces authorial interest in fusing the narrative, the descriptive, and the dramatic to illustrate the metaphorical journey toward the discovery of self.

For eighteenth-century describers of nature, the pictorial analogy was never distant. The cult of the picturesque dictated a schematic overlay through which the phenomenological world was seen often as ordered and domesticated, an attitude satirized slightly later by Jane Austen in this famous passage from *Northanger Abbey:*

> They were viewing the country with the eyes of persons accustomed to drawing, and decided on its capability of being formed into pictures, with all the eagerness of real taste. Here Catherine was quite lost. She knew nothing of drawing—nothing of taste:—and she listened to them with an attention which brought her little profit, for they talked in phrases which conveyed scarcely any idea to her. The little which she could understand however appeared to contradict the very few notions she had entertained on the matter before. It seemed as if a good view were no longer to be taken from the top of an high hill, and that a clear blue sky was no longer a proof of a fine day. She was heartily ashamed of her ignorance. (p. 137)[1]

Ann Radcliffe's descriptive writings often participate in this picturesque aesthetic. But she is technically innovative in at least one way that has failed until recently to attract much critical attention. She should occupy a place of honor in the development of the novel for incorporating extended visually oriented description into a dominantly narrative mode.

Radcliffe was one of the first English novelists to elevate extended, visually oriented landscape description—previously nearly the exclusive province of poetry—to a position of prominence in English fiction. In addition to establishing a new subject (subsequently developed by writers as diverse as Scott, Ruskin, Dickens, Hardy, Lawrence, and Woolf) she was the first to apply a genuinely cinematic technique to these descriptions. Obviously, Radcliffe knew nothing of modern cinematography, but her technique for capturing landscape in language closely resembles filmic "visualization through perspective" that combines object and seer.[2]

But Radcliffe only rarely achieves the consistency and kinetic effectiveness of a genuine word-painting. In her most famous work, *The Mysteries of Udolpho,* for example, descriptions mostly adhere to conventional stylistic eighteenth-century modes. Radcliffe's dominant descriptive mode presents static "catalogues" of elements in a landscape that are described in generalized, abstract terms and ordinarily rely heavily on contemporary formulas for the obligatory balancing of the sublime with the beautiful. The opening paragraph of the novel exemplifies such an approach.

On the pleasant banks of the Garonne, in the province of Gascony, stood, in the year 1584, the chateau of Monsieur St. Aubert. From its windows were seen the pastoral landscapes of Guienne and Gascony, stretching along the river, gay with luxuriant woods and vines, and plantations of olives. To the south, the view was bounded by the majestic Pyrenees, whose summits, veiled in clouds, or exhibiting awful forms, seen, and lost again, as the partial vapours rolled along, were sometimes barren, and gleamed through the blue tinge of air, and sometimes frowned with forests of gloomy pine, that swept downward to their base. These tremendous precipices were contrasted by the soft green of the pastures and woods that hung upon their skirts; among whose flocks, and herds, and simple cottages, the eye, after having scaled the cliffs above, delighted to repose. To the north, and to the east, the plains of Guienne and Languedoc were lost in the mist of distance; on the west, Gascony was bounded by the waters of Biscay. (p. 1)

A disembodied voice opens the novel by enumerating elements characteristic of a pastoral scene: gently winding river, noble mansion, cultivated slopes, and flocks grazing on soft green mountain pastures near the cottages of simple peasants. The identity of the observer is not important, and our ability to visualize the scene is hampered by the illogical perspective and the inert passivity of the language. Although there is a faint attempt to move our mental eye from the chateau to the Pyrenees to the south and then to north, east, and west in turn, it is impossible to understand how the observer can describe the chateau and the view from its windows simultaneously. The passive voice allows no rhythmic enlivening of the stilted, choppy phrases that built complex, often confusing, sentences. Verbs, adjectives, and adverbs lack specificity and color, but all elements contribute to depicting a natural landscape of peace and harmony between human beings and nature where "the eye after having scaled the cliffs above, delighted to repose" at an appropriately moderate mid-height.

The passage, though inert, introduces two favorite Radcliffian framing devices borrowed from the visual arts. We often find the heroine, Emily St. Aubert, gazing through a window onto a beautiful scene. This window helps to limit and organize what the observer sees; in addition, as in the passage above, a line of trees, a body of water, or the horizon line demarcates the farthest limit of her vision.

Radcliffe's dominant descriptive mode is characterized by descriptions of beautiful landscapes expressed in generalized diction that fails to capture their uniqueness. Her cinematic word-paintings, however, contrast vividly with the technique illustrated above. Her imagination, when thoroughly aroused by her concept of sublime landscape, struggles to free itself from generalized description to achieve an almost scientific particularity of observation. Not only does she include acute visual detail in such passages, but she also works out a kinetic technique to make the reader believe she or he sees the wild scenes she so obviously loved. Interestingly, Radcliffe's word-paintings represent the only places in *The Mysteries of Udolpho* where I sense the presence of a unique, impassioned voice. It is clearly the voice of Radcliffe herself.

There are five major word-paintings in *Udolpho* inserted among long narrative passages and briefer descriptive ones.[3] Their distribution may be structurally significant, for one important word-painting appears in each volume of the novel except for volume 3. A major cluster of extended landscape descriptions occurs in volume 2 and visualizes the heroine's journey through the Alps to Italy, her first brief look at Venice, and her journey through the Apennines to the Castle of Udolpho (a climactic moment in the complex plotting of the work). Through a close reading of the journey to Udolpho itself, I hope to demonstrate that, although we might consider Radcliffe shackled by the formulaic plots, characters, and themes of the Gothic tradition, she felt relatively freer than her male counterparts to explore the unknown territory of the cinematic word-painting and to contribute an innovative subject and technique to the English novel.

A brief sketch of the three major settings for Emily St. Aubert's literal and symbolic journey toward knowledge and happiness orients us to the complicated plot of *The Mysteries of Udolpho*. The novel begins in La Vallée, Emily's childhood home, where Emily lives harmoniously with nature in a version of the pastoral ideal, and no terrifying mysteries intrude. Although the author pays lip service to its picturesque beauties, the second major setting, the forbidding Castle of Udolpho, set amid the splendor and sublimity of the Alps, is the one that fully arouses the author's powers of description. This setting also provides the context for Emily's most lurid trials at the hands of the villainous Montoni. In the third setting, Chateau-le-Beau, Emily encounters her most sophisticated test, for she is required to discriminate between subtle manifestations of good and evil as the pastoral and gothic, the rational and irrational intermingle. Once Emily has learned to separate reality from illusion, her education is complete and her reward is marriage to the pallid, imperfect, but nonetheless lovable Valancourt.

At La Vallée the mountains and cliffs, safely remote, rim the horizon, providing a useful contrast with the cultivated valley. The light in this valley is clear, bright, and gay, permeated by soft greens and blues. But, as the recently orphaned Emily, her aunt, and the menacing Montoni (her aunt's new husband) journey through the Alps toward Montoni's castle, the landscape changes dramatically, as do the organizing mode of perception and the general level of intensity in the language. Here, finally, Radcliffe's writing achieves the sweep and vivid detail of a cinematic word-painting that distinguishes this mode from the static catalogue this essay previously examined.

Radcliffe's most successful word-painting begins: "At length, they reached a little plain, where the drivers stopped to rest the mules, whence a scene of such extent and magnificence opened below, as drew even from Madame Montoni a note of admiration" (p. 225). The passage organizes the dramatic ascent of the Alps as a progression through vistas—framed "scenes"—that provide suspense and offer Radcliffe the opportunity to describe pictorial motifs she had seen only in reproductions of popular paintings by Rosa, Claude, and Poussin at the time she described them here. Recurrent motifs borrowed from the cult of the picturesque include forbidding precipices and gnarled trees abutting tortuous narrow paths into high mountains with a pastoral landscape stretching into the mists below. Often—though not in the passage before us—other sense impressions augment the visual, such as the perfume of flowers or the faint sounds of lute, oboe, or violin music wafting up from some unknown source. This characteristic merging of sense impressions to heighten the moment's emotion anticipates a favorite strategy of Romantic poets and Victorian word-painters like Dickens and Tennyson.

As the little group of travellers ascends, magnificent panoramas dramatize the landscape by frequently reiterating contrasts between heights and depths and between enclosed and seemingly infinite space. More colorful and precise adjectives, adverbs, and verbs, a more coherent point of view, and a livelier sense of rhythm and movement replace the stilted language of La Vallée.

> Emily lost, for a moment, her sorrows, in the immensity of nature. Beyond the amphitheatre of mountains, that stretched below, whose tops appeared as numerous almost, as the waves of the sea, and whose feet were concealed by the forests—extended the Campagna of Italy, where cities and rivers, and woods and all the glow of cultivation were mingled in gay confusion. The Adriatic bounded the horizon, into which the Po and the Brenta, after winding through the whole extent of the landscape, poured their fruitful waves. (p. 225)

Moving from the foreground figures to the vista at their feet, "the immensity of nature" is made visible through language by the progressive description of mountain tops below the travellers and of the Italian countryside beyond, laid out in bird's-eye view. Vivid, active verbs such as stretch, mingle, bound, pour, in the following sentence sweep us along; and the syntactical rhythm echoes the speed of the eye as it takes in the variety of such a breathtaking scene.

Although she is hampered by mixed metaphors in the passage above, where visually confusing figurative clichés describe mountains as amphitheatre, ocean waves, and feet, Radcliffe's intention here is both bold and original. She is clearly stretching the linguistic medium to write movement into a description that progresses, as does a "camera eye," from mountain ranges to their tops, like waves, and, finally, to their bases in forests. A palpable excitement and intensity of language compensate for awkward figures of speech.

Three bodies of water both frame the vista and impart an additional sense of motion to the scene. The passage of time is signalled by the rather repetitious "at length," by which temporal progression implies spatial. The scene appears to be painted for the sheer joy of doing so, for, although the narrator realizes the magnificence of endlessly multiplying vistas, they only result in Emily's lassitude, loneliness, and fear. The last sentences of this passage, beginning "This pass," include the narrator's reference to "perspective" which again indicates her painterly orientation, as she tries to capture shifting forms caused by the changing perspective of the eye as it moves across a landscape.

> This pass, which led into the heart of the Apennine, at length opened to day, and a scene of mountains stretched in long perspective, as wild as any the travellers had yet passed. Still vast pine-forests hung upon their base, and crowned the ridgy precipice, that rose perpendicularly from the vale, while, above, the rolling mists caught the sun-beams, and touched their cliffs with all the magical colouring of light and shade. The scene seemed perpetually changing, and its features to assume new forms, as the winding road brought them to the eye in different attitudes; while the shifting vapours, now partially concealing their minuter beauties and now illuminating them with splendid tints, assisted the illusions of the sight. (pp. 225–26)

The final phrase of the passage—". . . the shifting vapours . . . assisted the illusions of the sight"—reminds us of Radcliffe's characteristic reliance on suggestive rather than explicit descriptive language when she is not word painting.

A later passage from this same word-painting in *The Mysteries of Udolpho* constitutes both its climax and the structural center of the novel, as the heroine journeys to the very heart of the Apennines. A fully realized cinematic panorama helps us visualize Emily's journey:

> Towards the close of day, the road wound into a deep valley. Mountains, whose shaggy steeps appeared to be inaccessible, almost surrounded it. To the east, a vista opened, that exhibited the Apennines in their darkest horrors; and the long perspective of retiring summits, rising over each other, their ridges clothed with pines, exhibited a stronger image of grandeur, than any that Emily had yet seen. The sun had just sunk below the top of the mountains she was descending, whose long shadow stretched athwart the valley, but his sloping rays, shooting through an opening of the cliffs, touched with a yellow gleam the summits of the forest, that hung upon the opposite steeps, and streamed in full splendour upon the towers and battlements of a castle, that spread its extensive ramparts along the brow of a precipice above. The splendour of these illumined objects was heightened by the contrasted shade, which involved the valley below.
> "There," said Montoni, speaking for the first time in several hours, "is Udolpho." (p. 226)

Here Radcliffe jams both light and compositional features into a single long sentence, as if straining to encapsulate kinetic motion through space in language's essentially static, temporal structure. Anticipating the Victorians' fondness for transitional moments at dusk or dawn where realities blur and the irrational may triumph, Radcliffe evokes the precise look of light on landscape as the sun sinks behind the mountains and the world darkens and chills.

Like James Thomson, famed for his descriptions of light, Radcliffe is interested in light effects. Unlike Thomson, however, she uses twilight to dramatize the climactic moment in the narrative when Emily first sees the picturesque and lurid castle, soon to be her prison. As she gazes "with melancholy awe" at Udolpho, the sloping rays of the sun shoot through, touch and stream with a splendor that contrasts with the encroaching shadows of night. In a momentary pause, Radcliffe carefully describes how the rays of the setting sun gradually travel up the castle wall to battlements and clustering towers, leaving behind "a melancholy purple tint" that foreshadows Emily's descent into darkness, cruelty, superstition, and terror. Significantly, at chapter's end, Emily, sitting at her window, can discern nothing in the darkness without. The next step in her education will depend on her learning to see and interpret both visual and psychological realities at Udolpho.

I am not the first to have noticed Ann Radcliffe's innovative novelistic technique. Indeed, Sir Walter Scott may have also been responding to this feature when he dubbed her "the first poetic novelist in English literature."[4] His comment implies the widespread assumption that narrative had hitherto been the dominant province of fiction and description that of poetry. Following Radcliffe's lead, Scott self-consciously includes word-paintings in novels such as *The Heart of Midlothian*. Early in the novel, he borrows both iconographical motifs and her organizing rationale (substituting "now" for "at length") to paint a prospect from Salisbury Crags outside of Edinburgh.

> If I were to choose a spot from which the rising or setting sun could be seen to the greatest possible advantage, it would be that wild path winding around the foot of the high belt of semicircular rocks, called Salisbury Crags, and marking the verge of the steep descent which slopes down into the glen on the south-eastern side of the city of Edinburgh. The prospect, in its general outline, commands a close-built, high-piled city, stretching itself out beneath in a form, which, to a romantic imagination, may be supposed to represent that of a dragon; now, a noble arm of the sea, with its rocks, isles, distant shores, and boundary of mountains; and now, a fair and fertile champaign country, varied with hill, dale, and rock, and skirted by the picturesque ridge of the Pentland mountains. But as the path gently circles around the base of the cliffs, the prospect, composed as it is of these enchanting and sublime objects, changes at every step, and presents them blended with, or divided from, each other, in every possible variety which can gratify the eye and the imagination. When a piece of scenery so beautiful, yet so varied,—so exciting by its intricacy, and yet so sublime,—is lighted up by the tints of morning or of evening, and displays all that variety of shadowy depth, exchanged with partial brilliancy, which gives character even to the tamest of landscapes, the effect approaches near to enchantment. (pp. 71–72)

But it was Scott's misfortune to suggest a comparison with Radcliffe's word-paintings, for, to my eye, his are derivative and pale compared to hers. Scott falls back on the mythologizing substructure (as in the comparison of the landscape to a dragon) nearly eschewed by Radcliffe in her most precise observations of nature. Not content to leave the underlying metaphor suggestive, he overwrites his point, concluding "the effect approaches near to enchantment."

Key words in this verbal visualization demonstrate Scott's dependence on a generalizing diction that tells us what the scene signifies but does not dramatize it vividly. In case we had missed it, Scott lets us know twice that the scene is a prospect, once that it is picturesque, twice each that it is beautiful, sublime, and appeals to "a romantic imagination." The serpentine organization of elements in this landscape and the dragon simile lend the description a fairy-tale quality that contrasts with Radcliffe's interest in objective description of phenomenological data in her narratives of landscape. Catherine Morland, the heroine of *Northanger Abbey,* would have had to be taught to visualize Scott's landscape in these terms. It would not have come naturally to her, any more than did Bath as picturesque landscape:

> A lecture on the picturesque immediately followed, in which his instructions were so clear that she soon began to see beauty in everything admired by him, and her attention was so earnest, that he became perfectly satisfied of her having a great deal of natural taste. He talked of fore-grounds, distances, and second distances—side-screens and perspectives— lights and shades;—and Catherine was so hopeful a scholar, that when they gained the top of Beechen Cliff, she voluntarily rejected the whole city of Bath, as unworthy to make part of a landscape. (p. 138)

In contrast to Austen's satire, another passage from *The Heart of Midlothian* illustrates Scott's dependence on conventional eighteenth-century diction to shape descriptions of the natural world. Toward the end of *Midlothian,* Effie, now Lady Staunton, walks with her nephew into the mountains to view a certain dramatic prospect. Although this episode constitutes the climactic meeting between Effie and her lost son, a sort of wolf-boy of the highlands, Scott, unlike Radcliffe, does not seize upon extended description of the wild scenery as a technique to signal the approaching climax.

> It was a walk of five long miles, and over rough ground, varied, however, and cheered, by mountain views, and peeps now of the firth and its islands, now of distant lakes, now of rocks and precipices. The scene itself, too, when they reached it, amply rewarded the labour of the walk. A single shoot carried a considerable stream over the face of a black rock, which contrasted strongly in colour with the white foam of the cascade, and, at the depth of about twenty feet, another rock intercepted the view of the bottom of the fall. The water, wheeling out far beneath, swept round the crag, which thus bounded their view, and tumbled down the rocky glen in a torrent of foam. (p. 524)

This passage demonstrates that Scott's primary interest is in naming landscape elements rather than dramatizing a narrative of landscape to be integrated with plot, character, and theme.

Like Radcliffe, Scott exhibits little interest in integrating narration with description. Both her Gothic narratives and his Romantic ones overwhelmingly participate in the eighteenth-century aesthetic preference for limiting the ecstasies and perils of the sublime with the orderliness of the beautiful and for the structural principle of alternating the modes of drama, narration and description. But, occasionally, when Radcliffe's imagination is aroused by the sublime, she reaches for a proto-Romantic descriptive technique where the emotions of the narrator—if not the protagonist—color the reporting of precise visual detail. At such moments, Radcliffe abandons generalized diction in favor of an aesthetic of particularity and passion, bringing her framed landscapes to life through a cinematic technique. This feature, passing through the fiction of Sir Walter Scott in a pale imitation of her visual precision, comes ultimately to rest in the novels of the greatest Victorian word-painter of them all, Charles Dickens, whose ability to fuse the modes of description and narration causes the natural world to become a correlative for the feelings and actions of characters. Examples of his consummate skill as word-painter await us next.

2

Dickens

*But may I not be forgiven for thinking it a wonderful testimony
to my being made for my art, that when, in the midst of this
trouble and pain, I sit down to my book, some beneficent power
shows it all to me and tempts me to be interested, and I don't
invent it—really do not—but see it, and write it down. . . .*
                                                    Dickens to Forster

Introduction

Dickens, whose novels date roughly half-way between those of Radcliffe and
Woolf, composes the most interesting word-paintings in the Victorian novel.
The epigraph above indicates the primacy of the visualizing imagination and
the painterly metaphor for this novelist. A sampling of representative descriptive passages in an early, middle, and late Dickens novel demonstrates a general movement from simple toward more complex ways of using word-paintings. In the early novel, *Barnaby Rudge* (1841), for example, Dickens is heavily dependent on the eighteenth-century rhetorical tradition and follows Walter
Scott's example in his use of the sublime to scene-paint for historical
panoramas. Picturesque schemata play a large role in the visual effects of this
novel.

   As Dickens masters his craft, however, he uses word-paintings in more
sophisticated ways which do not separate them from the body of the narrative
as in the earlier work. In a transitional novel like *David Copperfield* (1849–
50), Dickens begins to play with alternate points of view to the picturesque. He
reserves that older method of looking at landscape for the early fairy-tale passages in the novel, such as the descriptions of Peggotty's house. He also juxtaposes with that perspective an increasing reliance on more dramatized visualizations of characters utilizing the brief word-portrait and the verbal tableau.
Dickens's fascination with the theatre probably gives rise to his habit of
momentarily freezing the action, thereby creating a dramatic tableau. Dickens
uses this technique throughout his career to emphasize climactic events or, al-
ternately, to distance emotions stressful to characters—or to the narrator—by
the use of a static frame (usually an interior doorway or window).

The imagery and form of word-paintings written after 1850 sometimes symbolically prefigure changes in sensibilities of characters. Here, the movement of the major iconographic motif in *Little Dorrit* (1855–57) proves instructive. This late novel illustrates the progressively more symbolic ways in which Dickens uses word-paintings as he moves away from picturesque set-pieces and toward more sophisticated descriptive writing. We know from Dickens's monthly plans for the novel that he originally thought of the major visual motif as a rather stark and simple reiteration of the contrast between light and dark. But the author's evolving sense of the central experiences in the novel creates a changing imagery that seriously undercuts the optimistic intended meaning of its conclusion. Thus, attention to a recurrent visual element in *Little Dorrit* signals important changes in the sensibilities of either the main characters or— even more interestingly—in the narrator. In fact, evidence here suggests that the character may not be conscious of these changes at all! Word-painting in this novel assumes an intimate relationship with its narrative and themes and, therefore, contributes to a generally symbolic overall technique in descriptive writing. In *Little Dorrit,* it also may indicate that Dickens himself subtly altered the imagery to conform to his growing loss of confidence in the power of Christian love to solve individual problems.

Dickens greatly expands word-painting's repertory of subjects and effects as well as its relationship to the surrounding narrative. For this reason, he is centrally important to this study of Victorian word-painting. In general, visually composed description in Dickens develops in the direction of absorbing narrative and dramatic intent. But the development from picturesque to symbolic word-painting in Dickens represents no unmitigated progression, for even in his very last works, picturesque and symbolic word-paintings sometimes juxtapose. Nevertheless, one easily discerns the growing coherence among narrative, dramatic and descriptive modes in Dickens's novels. To put them between the word-paintings of Radcliffe and Woolf is to trace the progression toward fusing narrative and descriptive writing in the novel.

Barnaby Rudge: **Picturesque and Kinetic Word-Painting**

The generally neglected *Barnaby Rudge* (1841) is a particularly useful early work to consider because it draws so heavily upon Wordsworth and Scott.[1] In *Barnaby Rudge* Dickens also borrows heavily from the wild visionary set-pieces of Romantic writers such as Radcliffe and Byron. Like his predecessors, Dickens tends to moralize—sometimes, sentimentalize—natural landscapes in his early novels, thus domesticating their effect for a conservative, middle-class Victorian audience. My task in this chapter is to suggest the content and method of Dickensian word-painting by sampling representative passages from three novels in order to formulate what these extended descriptions contribute to new forms and uses for this feature. *Barnaby Rudge* is noteworthy because nearly one-third of its length is devoted to an enormously extended visually oriented description of the Gordon Riots and the burning of Newgate in 1780. Dickens solves two major aesthetic problems in this historical novel. First, he finds language to describe large historical actions in visual and kinetic terms; and second, he develops ways to integrate this diffuse material into an ongoing narrative. Critics, praising only the riot sections of *Barnaby Rudge,* suggest that Dickens solved the first problem rather better than the second. The present study intends to evaluate both aspects of this question.

The effect of the riots depends on the contrasting mood and setting of the novel's opening pages, which Dickens sets in a picturesque ancient country inn, the Maypole. This rural setting embodies a cluster of values Dickens characteristically associates with rural life: peace, beauty, Christian love, and reverence for the past—and these are precisely the values whose shredding constitutes the true horror of the riots. But the opening description of the Maypole offers no hint of the chaos soon to engulf city and country alike. Five long descriptive paragraphs open the novel, setting the stage for the first scene. This conventional eighteenth-century introduction borrows heavily from the earlier rhetorical tradition exemplified by Scott's *The Heart of Midlothian.* Scott's novel also opens with a large-scale set-piece describing the setting in which a broad historical panorama will take place, incorporates extensive scenes of mob violence, and centers much of the plot on a mentally deficient character.

But, whereas Scott's word-paintings reinforce the deliberate distancing of an elaborate narrative frame that emphasizes the pastness of the action, Dickens's word-painting of the Maypole—also a framing device for the narrative—is fresh and immediate. Our impression of vividness comes both from the accurate rendering of architectural details and from the underlying personification that organizes these details. The charm of this verbal visualization is realized in Cattermole's picturesque, delightful etchings of the Maypole in the first edition of *Barnaby Rudge,* admired by Dickens: "The Maypole was an old building, with more gable ends than a lazy man would care to count on a sunny day; huge zig-zag chimneys, out of which it seemed as though even smoke could not choose but come in more than naturally fantastic shapes, imparted to it in its tortuous progress; and vast stables, gloomy, ruinous, and empty" (p. 43). The description continues, after a brief digression to recount an apocryphal vignette about Queen Elizabeth's visit to the inn:

> The Maypole was really an old house, a very old house, perhaps as old as it claimed to be, and perhaps older, which will sometimes happen with houses of an uncertain, as with ladies of a certain age. Its windows were old diamond-pane lattices, its floors were sunken and uneven, its ceilings blackened by the hand of time, and heavy with massive beams. Over the doorway was an ancient porch, quaintly and grotesquely carved; and here on summer evenings the more favoured customers smoked and drank—ay, and sang many a good song too, sometimes—reposing on two grim-looking high-backed settles, which, like the twin dragons of some fairy tale, guarded the entrance to the mansion. (p. 44)

Dickens manages to work simultaneously in two directions here. First, he suggests the configurations of the Maypole so exactly that we can identify its architecture as either Tudor or Jacobean. At the same time, he begins to work his magic upon the inert building, transforming it into an artifact from the realm of the fantastic, whose roughness and generally irregular shapes suggest the eighteenth-century delight in the picturesque. The Maypole, with its large, rambling spaces and uneven roof lines immediately evokes an older, more magical agrarian England. Even the smoke emerging from its quaint chimneys assumes fantastic shapes, investing the passage with atmosphere and animation.

Legend augments fantasy as the narrator quickly digresses from the actual details of the building. In a lengthy aside, he alludes to its fabled origin in the reign of Henry VIII. He goes on to describe how Queen Elizabeth, visiting the Maypole, boxed the ears of her neglectful page. A wonderful analogue to the zig-zag outline of the chimneys, a similar design nicely characterizes the digressive nature of the narrative of *Barnaby Rudge,* which moves through many pages at a pace perhaps over-leisurely for the modern reader.

The extended description of the Maypole's tortuous progression of shapes sets the scene for the quaint inhabitants who grace its porches. But there is more than mere scene-setting here. We shall see how, as Dickens continues to perfect his art, he becomes progressively more interested in shaping description to contribute continuity and coherence to his novels. Yet, even as early as *Barnaby Rudge,* he invests word-painting with thematic meaning. Both digression into legend and the visually oriented Maypole descriptions suggest the dominant thematic motif for the novel: the clash between old and young. There are two major settings, and two kinds of people in this novel, and both reinforce this opposition. Throughout the novel, the bucolic, sentimentalized historic past of the Maypole and its environs—Olde England—contrasts with the chaotic energy of the present—Victorian London. And the peaceful quaint country folk live a life in utter contrast to the violence-prone citydwellers who will form the mob. Barnaby, the character who threads through this large historical canvas, is nearly an idiot; he is called a "natural" in the novel. He comes from a simpler rural England, and his fate represents a caricature of the innocent caught up in events he cannot understand.

The composition of the opening word-painting of the Maypole continues, after the Queen Elizabeth digression, with a passage describing the melange of sound that usually accompanies a fully realized set-description in Dickens. "Sparrows chirped and twittered," the air was alive with the "monotonous cooing" of pigeons and other birds which "suited . . . the grave and sober character of the building exactly, and seemed to lull it to rest" (p. 44). At this point the underlying personification begins to build until it achieves its full effect in the passage that follows.

With its overhanging stories, drowsy little panes of glass, and front bulging out and project-ing over the pathway, the old house looked as if it were nodding in its sleep. Indeed, it needed no very great stretch of fancy to detect in it other resemblances to humanity. The bricks of which it was built had originally been a deep dark red, but had grown yellow and discoloured like an old man's skin; the sturdy timbers had decayed like teeth; and here and there the ivy, like a warm garment to comfort it in its age, wrapt its green leaves closely round the time-worn walls.

It was a hale and hearty age though, still: and in the summer of autumn evenings, when the glow of the setting sun fell upon the oak and chestnut trees of the adjacent forest, the old house, partaking of its lustre, seemed their fit companion, and to have many good years of life in him yet. (p. 44)

The peacefulness of the general scene receives emphasis by comparing the old Maypole to a sleepy old man, aging slowly, wrapped harmoniously about with the protecting ivy. Dickens often uses personification to animate descriptions of buildings, sometimes turning an inert artifact into a lively "character" cameo. The impression of the Maypole is a happy one because the house, though gradually decaying, dwells in the midst of a "hale and hearty age" and, more importantly, exists in complete harmony with the natural world—the oaks and chestnuts—and the inevitable cycles of nature. "Glowing sunset" reinforces this impression. The narrator views this idyllic scene with affection, because it attests to the orderliness and stability of the natural framework. The word-painting relies, as does Thomson's *The Seasons,* on personification to unify de-tails. The salient change from the word-painting of Ann Radcliffe is the imag-inative transformation of the inert building to animated fantasy. And this pas-sage contributes to the development of Victorian word-painting by integrating descriptive details with thematic motifs in order to emphasize the contrast be-tween the old and the new, the past and the present.

Throughout the novel, the Maypole serves as a touchstone for the action. This site frames the entire novel, for its description opens the work, and the ac-tion concludes with the bloody duel between Chester and Haredale at Haredale's ruined country house near the Maypole itself. The inn physically survives the mob, but its spirit is shaken by violence, and its verities have been challenged.

As we shall later see, Dickens composes descriptions of London quite dif-ferently from this word-painting. Dickens exploits the visual elements of color, light, and dark in contrasting two backdrops for action. The attitude toward these two places remains constant: positive values abide in the country setting, where the Maypole stands "like some fairy tale" (p. 44). The city, on the other hand, resembles biblical Sodom and Gomorrah, which brimstone and fire de-stroyed. The word-paintings in *Barnaby Rudge,* which consistently invest the country with positive, and the city with negative, values, participate in narra-tive developments in this novel, though usually in a very heavy-handed way.

Like Radcliffe's *The Mysteries of Udolpho, Barnaby Rudge* alternates be-tween passages of extended description and those of narration and drama. The description of the Maypole, for example, precedes the opening scene, which introduces the reader to the landlord (John Willet) and to two ominous and mysterious strangers with shadowed faces, whose dark questions and hints generate the mysteries of the narrative.

In contrast to the picturesque word-painting of the Maypole, the vision of Gabriel Varden, traveling to London shortly after the novel's opening scene, foreshadows the kinetic descriptions of the city and mob. The locksmith receives a kind of prospect vision of the city,

> which lay outstretched before him like a dark shadow on the ground, reddening the sluggish air with a deep dull light, that told of labyrinths of public ways and shops, and swarms of busy people. Approaching nearer and nearer yet, this halo began to fade, and the causes which produced it slowly to develop themselves. Long lines of poorly lighted streets might be faintly traced, with here and there a lighter spot, where lamps were clustered round a square or market, or round some great building; after a time these grew more distinct, and the lamps themselves were visible; slight yellow specks, that seemed to be rapidly snuffed out, one by one, as intervening obstacles hid them from the sight. (p. 71)

This generally alarming view of London clearly opposes the cozy descriptive details of the Maypole. The reddish-yellow glow and the comparison of the city to "a dark shadow on the ground" evoke impressions of Hell, or, at least, of a modern valley of the shadow of death, where the air is decidedly unhealthy and the pilgrim walks in danger of losing his way amid labyrinthine streets. One notes the cinematic progression of the details in this description and the exceedingly precise observation of changing visual effects of light as Varden moves through the streets. Later I will compare this recording of light effects with the extended descriptions of cities that open Books I and II of *Little Dorrit* in order to trace Dickens's growing mastery of the fusion between narrative and descriptive modes. Again, sound follows visual impressions in this word-painting:

> Then, sounds arose—the striking of church clocks, the distant bark of dogs, the hum of traffic in the streets; then outlines might be traced—tall steeples looming in the air, and piles of unequal roofs oppressed by chimneys; then, the noise swelled into a louder sound, and forms grew more distinct and numerous still, and London—visible in the darkness by its own faint light, and not by that of Heaven—was at hand. (p. 71)

The description generates images of dull yellow lamps that illuminate nothing, then adding to them sounds of the city that neither soothe nor comfort. Where the terms of the Maypole description were fantastic, the city details are realistic; ugliness rather than beauty pervades the city, and no quaintness transforms the smoke from "unequal roofs oppressed by chimneys." The diction ("oppressed," "looming," "snuffed out") threatens rather than comforts. The underlying motif here is that of a journey in which man has lost his way in a kind of Hell, clearly out of harmony with nature and God.[2] This vision, with its alarming atmosphere, helps prepare the reader for the mob violence and general conflagration soon to commence in this hellish place.

Thus, even relatively early in his career, Dickens carefully uses extended visually oriented descriptions both to suggest the moral poles of the narrative, and to foreshadow themes he will explore. The opposition between the Maypole and London prompts us to interpret the meaning of the riots and the burning of Newgate more clearly than do the rather uninteresting adventures of the characters themselves.

Preparing to compose the riot scene, Dickens well understood the aesthetic problems involved in capturing chaos in language and in relating description to character development and narration. In a letter to John Landseer (5 November 1841), Dickens comments upon the proper technique for describing the large movements of a riot:

> I need not tell you who are so well acquainted with 'Art' in all its forms, that in the description of such scenes, a broad, bold, hurried effect must be produced, or the reader instead of being forced and driven along by imaginary crowds will find himself dawdling very uncomfortably through the town, and greatly wondering what may be the matter. In this kind of work the object is,—not to tell everything, but to select the striking points and beat them into the page with a sledge-hammer. . . . my object has been to convey an idea of multitudes, violence, and fury; and even to lose my own dramatis personae in the throng, or only see them dimly, through the fire and smoke. (Appendix, pp. 739–40)

Dickens accurately saw that in order to convey his "striking points . . . an idea of multitudes, violence, and fury," he needed a carefully selective descriptive technique and a deliberate de-emphasis of character. The resulting riot descriptions lend both strength and weakness to the overall composition of the novel.

The novel is chiefly memorable for the visual immediacy of the climactic riot scenes, which explode over two hundred pages of the novel. Here, Dickens captures a panorama of wildly shifting action that Gordon Spence and other critics praise for "an ability, which has seldom been equalled, to describe the movement of crowds in the states of agitation and riot."[3] On the other hand, Dickens destroys the unity of his narration by letting the description exfoliate over eighteen chapters. The extended—and climactic—descriptions of mob violence cause the first forty-eight chapters to seem mere prelude to the events of the riots, leaving the author only eight chapters in which to conclude the novel. The work, in essence, lacks balance.

Although the novel lacks overall coherence, however, *Barnaby Rudge* is important to our study of word-painting because it reveals Dickens trying to work out the relationships between narrative, dramatic, and descriptive modes. As he fears in the letter just quoted, he does lose his dramatic personae (who are none too clearly delineated to begin with). The canvas is full of quickly sketched characters, typical of historical novels, and even the main characters fail to develop.

The major failure appears where success is most needed: the figure of Barnaby himself. Supposedly the center of interest, Barnaby fluctuates between being the noble hero—who is also the fool—and being merely the village idiot. Intended—from title to conclusion—to mirror a chaotic, broad narrative, Barnaby's slender intelligence cannot carry the burden of meaning, and most times he only befuddles himself and tires the reader.

Nonetheless, in de-emphasizing the characters, Dickens puts the riots themselves in the center of our minds, and gives his astonishing powers of visualization full play. His brilliant descriptive writing constitutes the novel's true greatness. One might even claim that the riots themselves preempt the functions of character, and that their descriptions incorporate both narrative and dramatic modes. Such a claim would constitute a new use for word-painting. But the extensive descriptions of riots, incorporating several major word-paintings, fail to integrate well with the overall structure of the novel. They go on too long, and tend to overwhelm the novel's other elements.

The word-paintings, however, do succeed in two major ways. First, simply as a tour de force of descriptive writing, they are nearly unequalled in Dickens's œuvre. They also sustain both visual and thematic coherence within themselves even though they are only imperfectly integrated with the rest of the narrative.

Six chapters describing the genesis of the riots introduce descriptive elements and connect them to the visual motifs established in Varden's early vision of London. Thus, the "deep dull light" that reddens the sluggish air ultimately erupts into the torches that destroy both London and the countryside. The contrast between light and dark provides the major element in the descriptions, sometimes strikingly melodramatic as faces suddenly illuminate in the surrounding darkness. The use of light and dark in this novel is consistent, simplistic, and often overdone. Golden light stands for goodness and always illuminates Barnaby, even when he is standing in the den of evil, whereas the mob and its villainous leaders always appear in shadows, or in the darkness of evil and ignorance: "To Hugh and his companion, who lay in a dark corner of the gloomy shed, he (Barnaby), and the sunlight, and the peaceful Sabbath sound to which he made response, seemed like a bright picture framed by the door, and set off by the stable's blackness" (p. 478). Barnaby often appears in this context: framed by a door or window that puts him in another place and time from his evil companions. His madness is innocent where theirs is deliberate, and therefore wrong. Note how self-consciously Dickens employs commonplace pictorial motifs in the passage just quoted, one of many examples in *Barnaby Rudge* where visually oriented descriptions remind Dickens of "bright pictures." This novel also contains "a series of pictures representing the streets of London in the night" (chapter 16), and a reference to Gabriel's triumphant return to the Maypole as "a bright picture" (p. 713).

The terms of these descriptions indicate that at many points in *Barnaby*

Rudge, Dickens thought like a painter. *Little Dorrit* demonstrates how much more subtly Dickens uses the visual motifs of light and darkness in later novels where they carry meaning that often undercuts the asserted intention of the narrative, and even when they support the optimistic intended meaning, support it in a far more ambiguous manner.

A second iconographic element common to descriptions of the mob and Varden's vision of London emerges from Varden's sense of London as Hell. Though Varden knows that the oddly unnatural light by which he first sees the city derives from an artificial source, Dickens suggests a religious connotation in the phrase, "visible in the darkness by its own faint light, and not by that of Heaven" (p. 71). If not Heaven, then surely Hell. In every climactic passage of the riot descriptions—and especially in those describing the destruction of the Maypole, the Warren, and Newgate—Dickens emphasizes the demonism of the rioters and demonstrates their mad behavior. The mob floods the streets as would a sea or a river, filling the bewildering labyrinth like some maddened natural force. Fire and blood—the red colors of Hell—provide leitmotifs for the descriptions of terrifying events and frightful sounds. Throughout this section of the novel, again and again the narrator alludes to the hallucinatory nature of what the eye sees: a nightmare vision that comes and goes with the unreality of a dream.

Several examples must stand here for the many descriptions that constitute the internally coherent word-paintings studding the story of the riots. As the first days of the riot unfold, Gashford, the diabolical mastermind who does Chester's bidding, looks down from the upper window of a house in which he has taken refuge at the crowds he has incited:

> Thus—a vision of coarse faces, with here and there a blot of flaring, smoky light; a dream of demon heads and savage eyes, and sticks and iron bars uplifted in the air, and whirled about; a bewildering horror in which so much was seen, and yet so little, which seemed so long, and yet so short, in which there were so many phantoms, not to be forgotten all through life, and yet so many things that could not be observed in one distracting glimpse—it flitted onward, and was gone. (p. 465)

Again, we have the opposition of "vision" and "dream," of sharply perceived detail and hallucination, of demonism in the "flaring, smoky light," and the suggestive rapidity of movement that one both sees and does not see at moments of crisis. This passage reflects the complex syntax of Dickens's mob descriptions, its staccato rhythms, and the nightmare distortions of time that freezes the action for a brief moment.

Point of view provides the reader with essential orientation within such kinetic passages so she can visualize the scene completely. In this scene, Gashford provides us with a fixed point, above the crowd, from which to view the action. Dickens often uses this vantage point to frame action through the eyes of a physically removed observer who looks down from a window upon the phantasmic shapes of the mob and records them for us. When the mob marches upon the Maypole shortly thereafter, the landlord, John Willet, performs a similar narrative function by providing a still-point toward which the crowd moves.

The descriptions of both the Maypole and the Warren mark the climaxes in the long description of the riots. Having already vividly seen the madness of the mob vandalizing London's Catholic churches (which it detests), one knows that its fearful powers cannot be stopped by simple, naive, peaceful country folk. And, while the height of horrific destruction constitutes the second climax, the burning of Newgate, our emotional response to the attack on the Maypole is much more intense because of the affection with which the narrator has described the rural setting and its inhabitants. The attack, again, is framed, this time by the idyll of peaceful country life.

John Willet has just wakened from a nap on a quiet summer's eve. Then, in two brief paragraphs the scene changes from the bucolic picturesque setting to one of kinetic mayhem:

> When he awoke, the rich light had faded, the sombre hues of night were falling fast upon the landscape, and a few bright stars were already twinkling overhead. The birds were all at roost, the daisies on the green had closed their fairy hoods, the honeysuckle twining round the porch exhaled its perfume in a twofold degree, as though it lost its coyness at that silent time and loved to shed its fragrance on the night; the ivy scarcely stirred its deep green leaves. (p. 494)

Interestingly enough, Dickens makes us *see* this scene by describing it in terms only glancingly visual. Instead, the melange of sense impressions builds a coherent word-painting eliciting (in Gombrick's term) available picturesque schemata to construct fragmented sense impressions into a mental picture. As in the opening description of the Maypole, the elements of the landscape demonstrate bird sounds, the perfumed fragrances of flowers, and enveloping green ivy to generate a general feeling of domestic well-being and harmony. But this is the last time we are to hear about the enchantedness of the Maypole; soon it will be fairyland no more. For into this tranquil scene a new sound announces the intrusion of the contemporary world:

> Was there no sound in the air, besides the gentle rustling of the trees and the grasshopper's merry chirp? Hark! Something very faint and distant, not unlike the murmuring in a sea-shell. Now it grew louder, fainter now, and now it altogether died away. Presently, it came again, subsided, came once more, grew louder, fainter—swelled into a roar. It was on the road, and varied with its windings. All at once it burst into a distinct sound—the voices, and the tramping feet of many men. (p. 494)

This passage develops the primary analogy between the mob and the sea, which commences in a famous comment by the narrator as the mob begins to form:

A mob is usually a creature of very mysterious existence, particularly in a large city. Where it comes from or whither it goes, few men can tell. Assembling and dispersing with equal suddenness, it is as difficult to follow to its various sources as the sea itself; nor does the parallel stop here, for the ocean is not more fickle and uncertain, more terrible when roused, more unreasonable, or more cruel. (p. 475)

The sea image, which is present in practically every single description of the mob in *Barnaby Rudge,* contributes to the coherence of Dickens's visualizations of the mob, its shapelessness and random violence. Like the sea, the sounds of the mob, described above, swell and recede as the mob advances toward dull-witted John Willet, who will be changed forever by its arrival. The shifting sounds document the aural dimension of the word-painting as accurately as it records the look of the approaching mob. Both build a cinematic sense of rapid, disorienting movement in a previously static scene.

The mob arrives so quickly at the Maypole that, like John Willett, we are bewildered by the event; we cannot really assimilate it, lending it the unreality of a terrible dream: "A dark mass, looming through a cloud of dust, soon became visible; the mob quickened their pace; shouting and whooping like savages, they came rushing on pell-mell; and in a few seconds he was bandied from hand to hand, in the heart of a crowd of men" (p. 495). The vivid action verbs, piled one after another, register rapid movement. We view the events from Willet's perspective while he waits helplessly to be overrun. As he stares, the descriptive pace quickens, and Dickens gives us another word-painting that freezes action at a moment of utter horror and numbness, an attempt to contain movement and chaos whose terrors are too intense for expression: "John stared round at the mass of faces—some grinning, some fierce, some lighted up by torches, some indistinct, some dusky and shadowy: some looking at him, some at his house, some at each other—and while he was, as he thought, in the very act of doing so, found himself, without any consciousness of having moved, in the bar . . ." (p. 497). Clipped phrases, strung together in a rhythm of repeated syntactic structures ("some . . . some," for example) accurately reflect Willet's inability to assimilate the assault upon his beloved Maypole. This passage, only half of a single long sentence that represents a paragraph of text, illustrates Dickens's characteristic syntax for kinetic descriptions. As Willet looks from face to face, we see, with him, the stark contrasts between lighted and unlighted areas of this word-painting and the constantly shifting composition of the figures. We glimpse fragments of suggestive, threatening facial expressions and gestures that indicate exactly how Dickens visualizes the scene. At the same time, the word-painting benefits from the fixed perspective from which we can view the chaos. By showing this from Willet's viewpoint, we grasp his emotional paralysis simultaneously involved and detached.

The description of the vandalizing of the Maypole bar comes to its climax in the paragraph following the one we have just examined. Dickens paradoxically achieves an effect of kinesis by freezing a selected number of visual phenomena. The sacred Maypole is violated by the mob; its sacredness is both absurd and consistent with Willet's perspective. The syntax quickens even more as we feel the terror or random, mindless violence.

> Yes. Here was the bar—the bar that the boldest never entered without special invitation—the sanctuary, the mystery, the hallowed ground: here it was, crammed with men, clubs, sticks, torches, pistols; filled with a deafening noise, oaths, shouts, screams, hootings; changed all at once into a bear-garden, a mad-house, an infernal temple: men darting in and out, by door and window, smashing the glass, turning the taps, drinking liquor out of China punchbowls, sitting astride of casks, smoking private and personal pipes, cutting down the sacred grove of lemons, hacking and hewing at the celebrated cheese, breaking open inviolable drawers, putting things in their pockets which didn't belong to them, dividing his own money before his own eyes, wantonly wasting, breaking, pulling down and tearing up: nothing quiet, nothing private: men everywhere—above, below, overhead, in the bedrooms, in the kitchen, in the yard, in the stables—clambering in at windows when there were doors wide open; dropping out of windows when the stairs were handy; leaping over the bannisters into chasms of passages: new faces and figures presenting themselves every instant—some yelling, some singing, some fighting, some breaking glass and crockery, some laying the dust with the liquor they couldn't drink, some ringing the bells till they pulled them down, others beating them with pokers till they beat them into fragments: more men still—more, more, more—swarming on like insects: noise, smoke, light, darkness, frolic, anger, laughter, groans, plunder, fear, and ruin! (p. 497)

This is the best example from *Barnaby Rudge* of Dickens's technique for rendering kinetic action through the essentially frozen medium of verbal word-paintings. Utilizing a visual orientation that resembles cinematic technique, a single-sentence paragraph, a tour de force of descriptive writing, gradually accumulates increasingly dramatic details into itself in a quickly accelerating rhythm of repeated nouns, verbs, and prepositions. Frantic, fragmented action finds its stylistic analogue in gradually shortening phrases and a crescendo of speed. Phrases are cut off, replaced by brief catalogues of actions and sense impressions. A darting movement directs the mind's eye from one section of the room to the other to make us feel that we are moving through the interior of the Maypole in a blur of present participles and active verbs to connote incompleted actions. By means of such linguistic structures augmented by quick sketches and discrete images, we receive a vivid sense of the speed and confusion of the scene.

Frenzied though this word-painting is, its placement in the structure of the novel also tells us about Dickens's preference for framing a potentially uncontrollable scene. The point of view of a quiescent observer gives us a still-point from which to grasp the shifting panorama. In later Dickens novels, this effect will not be so easy for the writer to accomplish, as we shall note in the clash between intended meaning and subtext in the enigmatic ending to *Little Dorrit*.

Dickens's description of the violation of the Maypole bar adds a new and important dimension to our general sense of the possibilities for word-painting, for it relies heavily for its effects of mass movement on a kinetic and impressionistic dynamic vastly different from the effects of the set-pieces and early word-paintings we have examined thus far. Like earlier word-paintings, Dickens's occur at climactic moments in the narrative. But in contrast to the earlier visually oriented descriptions, the narrator's attitude toward both rioters and riots—and the way in which he describes them—reflects the values and themes of the novel as a whole.

Like the other Dickensian word-paintings we have noted so far, the aural element immediately joins the visual to create a fully realized and dramatic word-painting. As the mob, having left the Maypole in shambles "like the bow spit of a wrecked ship" (p. 500), begins to flood through the Warren, a fearful alarm bell begins to toll. The narrator informs us that this unearthly "bell . . . speaks the language of the dead" (p. 504), that it is "the wrathful voice of God" (p. 505). While the writing here is too forced—a "Dies Irae" that does not emerge naturally from the terms of the description is imposed on the scene—sound once again contributes to the visualization of Dickens's word-painting and demonstrates the additive structure of such passages.

Several pages describing the wasting of the Warren culminate in the grotesquerie of the concluding vignette, where the behavior of the rioters reaches its orgiastic height.

> If Bedlam gates had been flung wide open, there would not have issued forth such maniacs as the frenzy of that night had made. . . . There were men who cast their lighted torches in the air, and suffered them to fall upon their heads and faces, blistering the skin with deep unseemly burns. . . . On the skull of one drunken lad—not twenty, by his looks—who lay upon the ground with a bottle to his mouth, the lead from the roof came streaming down in a shower of liquid fire, white hot; melting his head like wax. (p. 508)

And then, suddenly as it arrived, the mob has gone, and silence descends upon the scene. Silence, stasis, and darkness designate closure for these terrible scenes: "A dull smoke hung upon the ruin, as though to hide it from those eyes of Heaven; and the wind forbore to move it. Bare walls, roof open to the sky— chambers, where the beloved dead had, many and many a fair day, risen to new life and energy . . ." (p. 508). Just as the chapter began with the fairy-tale sleep of John Willet, so it closes with "the silence and solitude of utter desolation" (p. 509). Thus, Dickens frames the fearful events and disquieting emotions of the riots with a wider, cosmic perspective that returns us to order and peace, if not to peace of mind.

The second climax in the riot description, the firing of Newgate, comes one hundred pages later in the text. I shall not examine these passages involving the Newgate in detail because they add nothing new to this discussion of Dickens's descriptive technique in *Barnaby Rudge*. But it is instructive to note the relative weight given to the riot descriptions and the narrative of the characters' fortunes in this section of the novel. A total of eighteen chapters describes the two major events of the riots. In between two essentially similar high points of description, seven chapters ramble through an accounting of Haredale, who arrests Barnaby's father in the smoking ruins of the Warren, and Barnaby's arrest at the villains' hideout. Barnaby and his father happen to meet in the same jail cell, where father confesses his cruel deeds and son and father are reconciled on the eve of their intended public execution, which is subsequently thwarted when the rioters free the prisoners from Newgate. In the meantime, the evil Hugh torments his angelic prisoners, Emma and Dolly, with threats of bodily harm, but is distracted from his sport by the march upon Newgate.

Clearly, this is a surfeit of action for a mere seven chapters. It crams an extensive summary of action involving many different characters into a small space and is sandwiched by the drawn-out climactic descriptions of the rioters at the Maypole, the Warren, and Newgate. Here is proof that the narrative interest in this novel is carried by the extended riot descriptions, for the descriptive passages have a care and weight to their expression unmatched by the sketchy characters and plot of the supposedly narrative chapters.

In *Barnaby Rudge,* Dickens invests word-paintings with themes and narrative movement. He introduces cinematic movement into these extended visualizations, yet keeps them orderly by framing them both with narrative materials and the point of view of an observer. And he incorporates both narrative and dramatic matters into the descriptions which constitute the dominant mode in the climactic quarter of this long novel. Yet, most readers finish this novel basically unsatisfied because, while the writer achieves his goal of suggesting "multitudes, violence and fury" (letter to Landseer), he loses the narrative shape of the novel along the way, and does not give us fully developed characters to match the depth of his descriptive sections.

Dickens faces an aesthetic problem in *Barnaby Rudge* that is similar to the one Virginia Woolf would face in her "prosepoems" a half-century later. How does one capture the flux of events that change through time in a fixed verbal continuum? Moreover, how does one integrate this descriptive material into the narrative and dramatic emphasis of the British novel? Dickens solves the first problem brilliantly in *Barnaby Rudge,* as we have seen. But, Dickens, whose point of view remains omniscient, does not have the possibility of Woolf's "stream" technique. In early novels like *Barnaby Rudge,* Dickens does not consistently solve the problem of giving an aesthetically pleasing shape to the integration of description and narration. The word-paintings themselves, however, possess a sophisticated inner coherence; they also help us locate the values implicit in rural and urban settings in this novel. Word-paintings work in *Barnaby Rudge* because they are invested with narrative meanings and often assume a character of their own. And the riots themselves occasionally develop into fully cinematic word-paintings.

Dickens, who uses these visually oriented descriptions to dramatize mob horror, demonstrates his well-documented terror of social breakdown and chaos. The imagery of the city in *Barnaby Rudge* also suggests the writer's fear of the city with its hellish connotations. Word-paintings carry a simple moral in this novel: social chaos is evil and has no redeeming features. Yet, may we as readers of word-paintings be forgiven if we find the riot descriptions more interesting—because they are more lively and dramatic—than the picturesque "view-hunting" that produces the descriptions of the Maypole, where time stands still?

David Copperfield: Word-Portraits and Verbal Tableaux

The interesting kinetic word-paintings in *Barnaby Rudge* and their relationship to the narrative offer us a baseline with which to compare Dickens's subsequent treatment of visually oriented descriptions. An examination of *David Copperfield* (1849–50) reveals an emerging pattern in this writer's development of word-painting. First, the basic content of extended, visually oriented descriptions shifts rather sharply. Gone—with two important exceptions to be discussed later—are the long sublime or picturesque set pieces so prevalent in both eighteenth-century novelistic descriptions and the early work of Dickens. In place of them, *David Copperfield* increasingly relies on two other types of word-painting, whose subject matter is character rather than setting.

The first—which we shall call word-portraiture—descends from the seventeenth-century tradition of "characters," in which an author quickly sketches a variety of representative character "types" in a series of brief prose vignettes. Although hardly new to Dickens—see, for example, Gabriel Varden's word-portrait in *Barnaby Rudge,* or, earlier, those in *Sketches by Boz* and *Pickwick Papers*—Dickens puts word-portraiture to particularly effective use in *David Copperfield,* thus justifying our examination of the motif in this novel of Dickens's middle period. The second gives us frozen scenes, dramatic moments of climax in the lives of the characters, or in the progress of the narrative.

These scenes—verbal analogues to the immensely popular "tableaux vivants" of the Victorian period[4]—are carefully composed, often according to the schemata that have concerned us in earlier chapters of this study. They are heavily visual in emphasis, are usually framed by doorway or window, and gain visual coherence from a clear placement of the spectator. These are often the scenes chosen for illustration by Dickens's artist-collaborators in early editions of the novels. Although their painterly approach resembles that of the earlier word-paintings we have examined, their subjects vastly differ. Again, though *Pickwick Papers* may employ tableaux even more prominently, examining the motif in *David Copperfield* allows us to demonstrate Dickens's increasing reliance on word-portraits and verbal tableaux, and also to evaluate how effectively these forms integrate with narration.

The shift in emphasis of word-paintings in *David Copperfield* signals a change in the relationship between word-painting and narrative in Dickens. The critic Jerome Thale considers Dickens "*the* great symbolic novelist."[5] Furthermore, he finds description to be the very foundation of Dickens's symbolic art. A chronological study of Dickens's fiction indicates that this writer became increasingly interested in tightening up the continuity of his large-scale novels. A greater dependency on symbolic technique shows up in the descriptive detail of novels beginning with *David Copperfield*.[6] Therefore, a study of the growing intimacy between word-paintings and the concerns of narrative helps us see exactly how this evolution toward novels with greater internal coherence occurs.

Critics agree that *David Copperfield* represents a transitional work in the Dickens canon for, although its tone remains generally optimistic, the novels that come after it paint a more pessimistic picture of the individual and society. *David Copperfield,* always Dickens's favorite creation, transmutes often-painful autobiographical materials into an idealized fairy tale of his life, in which love redeems the past. The first-person narrator sets a generally sympathetic tone, as he looks back nostalgically over his life and rarely comments upon his childhood foibles. A decade later, when Dickens reworks some of these same materials into *Great Expectations,* a different, more ironic narrative stance yields a much darker novel and much more ambiguous word-paintings and patterns of imagery.

Although *David Copperfield* is transitional in several ways, it interests us here primarily because of the juxtaposition of picturesque descriptions of settings with more dramatic verbal visualizations of characters. In general, Dickens saves the picturesque mode for those scenes of early childhood that nearly every reader of *David Copperfield* fondly recalls for their ability to conjure up the magic of a child's vision. This point of view organizes roughly the first quarter of the novel, particularly David's earliest memories of life with his mother and Peggotty's private world. The magic derives in part from the picturesque word-paintings that color the first section of the novel, transmuting ordinary facts into fairy tales.

Dickens relies on picturesque schemata in the account of David's childhood. But—even more interestingly—this mode of description almost entirely disappears once David has fled from the servitude of Murdstone and Grinby for the safety of Aunt Betsy Trotwood's in Dover. Many readers have felt that the novel loses intensity after this first section; this reaction may partly be due to the more diffuse quality of both narrative and descriptive materials in the rest of the novel.

As David matures, he appears to outgrow his ability to compose the past into a series of comforting visually organized pictures that rely on the perspective of nostalgia. Significantly, the only other picturesque descriptions in the novel—none of which take the form of true word-paintings but only resemble snippets of description—center either on David's courtship of and marriage to Dora or occur in the four retrospective chapters that periodically summarize the narrative to that point. In both cases, the narrator must learn to move beyond past errors to achieve maturity. A striking pattern in Dickens's placement of word-paintings emerges: picturesque landscape descriptions in this novel occur only in David's reminiscences of childhood, or of childlike episodes in his life. The only sublime, extended Alpine description in this novel à la Radcliffe or Wordsworth operates as catalyst for David's revelation concerning the true nature of his feelings for Agnes, and signals his increasingly realistic relationship toward the world of the present.

In place of romanticized, schematic pictures from the past, *David Copperfield* increasingly turns to the two kinds of symbolic word-paintings—word-portraits and verbal tableaux—to which we have already referred. In a wonderful stylistic analogue to David's improving insight into the true nature of things, both of these new kinds of word-paintings dominate the latter two-thirds of the novel. In order to demonstrate this strategy the present chapter will offer examples of picturesque word-painting (the description of Peggotty's boat, Aunt Betsy's house, the Wickfields), word-portraiture (Ham, Miss Murdstone, and Uriah Heep), and verbal tableaux (Emily on the plank, and Annie and Dr. Strong at home). These examples show both the increasingly organic relationship between word-painting and its surrounding narrative and the development of new subjects and techniques for word-paintings themselves.

In the early section of *David Copperfield,* Dickens's descriptive method is highly reminiscent of the Maypole descriptions we have just examined. But a comparison between the opening chapters of *Barnaby Rudge* and *David Copperfield* indicates that Dickens's interest has shifted from historical panorama and descriptions of setting to characterization and descriptions colored by the point of view of the narrator. The heavily subjective nature of the visualizations in the opening chapters of *David Copperfield* make for a more dynamic generation of narrative than was true of *Barnaby Rudge.*

The outstanding example of picturesque word-painting in *David Copperfield*—and perhaps in all of Dickens—is the extended description of Peggotty's house. Ham walks toward the house with David, who sees only a battered boat.

> "Yon's our house, Mas'r Davy!"
> I looked in all directions, as far as I could stare over the wilderness, and away at the sea, and away at the river, but no house could *I* make out. There was a black barge, or some other kind of superannuated boat, not far off, high and dry on the ground, with an iron funnel sticking out of it for a chimney and smoking very cosily; but nothing else in the way of a habitation that was visible to *me.* (p. 31)[7]

The education of David's vision begins here, with this external view of Peggotty's house. In the process of his journey through life he must learn to see what is really there, instead of romanticizing and idealizing all phenomena. As he explores this unconventional home, he begins to recognize that home can be found in the most unlikely settings, and a gentle and charming corrective to stereotyped vision commences.

As was the case in the picturesque Maypole description, the narrator here communicates a sense of childhood wonder in the freshness and delight with which he recalls the interior details of the houseboat.

> If it had been Aladdin's palace, roc's egg and all, I suppose I could not have been more charmed with the romantic idea of living in it. There was a delightful door cut in the side, and it was roofed in, and there were little windows in it; but the wonderful charm of it was, that it was a real boat, which had no doubt been upon the water hundreds of times, and which had never been intended to be lived in, on dry land. . . .
>
> It was beautifully clean inside, and as tidy as possible. There was a table, and a Dutch clock, and a chest of drawers, and on the chest of drawers there was a tea-tray with a painting on it of a lady with a parasol, taking a walk with a military-looking child who was trundling a hoop. The tray was kept from tumbling down by a Bible; and the tray, if it had tumbled down, would have smashed a quantity of cups and saucers and a teapot that were grouped around the book. On the walls there were some common coloured pictures, framed and glazed, of Scripture subjects; such as I have never seen since in the hands of pedlars, without seeing the whole interior of Peggotty's brother's house again, at one view. Abraham in red going to sacrifice Isaac in blue, and Daniel in yellow cast into a den of green lions, were the most prominent of these. (pp. 31–32)

Similar to the fairy-tale context for the Maypole, the suggestion of a parallel with Aladdin's palace begins the work of transforming an admittedly fanciful structure into a magical setting. It is a child's dream come true. At the same time that the language suggests the intensity of sense impressions to a young child, the objects in the boat are accurately enumerated so that we are convinced that such a place could really exist. The child's eye provides a coherent point of view by means of which to move logically from one item that strikes him to the next, and the things David notices are the things we would expect a child to notice: furniture, tea things, Bible, and narrative art work painted in vivid colors. But mostly David is captivated by the diminished scale of this house ("little windows," and later in the description, his own "little window," and "little bed"), and the whole fantastic idea of metamorphosis: that a boat could be a house.

What at first appears to be a random catalogue of objects in this word-painting reveals a carefully thought-out relationship to narrative and theme. First, the furnishings and art in the Peggotty's home suggest their social and economic status and their value system. Neatness, cleanliness, and piety are dominant notes. In addition, the pictures on the wall can be "read" in the same way Victorians read genre paintings and found typological significance in the Old Testament. For example, one picture represents Daniel in the lion's den (p. 31). This illustration foreshadows Daniel Peggotty's search through the wide world to recover his "fallen" niece. He visits the most dangerous haunts of criminals and prostitutes, yet emerges from his travels unscathed. The suggestion is that God, Peggotty's own innate goodness, and his love for Emily are sufficient protection from evil. This example shows how seemingly random descriptive details in the picturesque word-paintings of *David Copperfield*—unlike those details of the Maypole in *Barnaby Rudge*—suggest narrative figurations and specific themes to come in the novel.

The visually coherent imaginary tour of the houseboat continues as Peggotty shows David to his own bedroom.

> It was the completest and most desirable bedroom ever seen—in the stern of the vessel; with a little window, where the rudder used to go through; a little looking-glass, just the right height for me, nailed against the wall, and framed with oyster-shells; a little bed, which there was just enough room to get into; and a nosegay of seaweed in a blue mug on the table. The walls were white-washed as white as milk, and the patchwork counterpane made my eyes quite ache with its brightness. One thing I particularly noticed in this delightful house was the smell of fish, which was so searching that when I took out my pocket-handkerchief to wipe my nose, I found it smelt exactly as if it had wrapped up a lobster. (p. 32)

The simple lines and the bright, primary colors of this word-painting convey the child's sense of how someone's aesthetic has transformed an ordinary boat into an enchanted place. The clarity of the composition and the absence of somber tones initiate an underlying sense that there are essentially two worlds in *David Copperfield*. As in *Barnaby Rudge,* the country characteristically represents the world of feelings, love, security, and beauty; and the working world of the city forces people to suppress feelings in favor of the intellect, self-serving motives, insecurity, and a strictly utilitarian environment.[8] Peggotty's houseboat offers both physical and psychological refuge for David, a lonely, helpless child, and protects him for a time against the hostile world of the Murdstones.

The boat also offers protection from the hostile sea whose violence will overpower Ham at the climax of the novel. In what we have come to expect as the extension of visual word-paintings into the aural dimension, our word-painting of Peggotty's home adds sound and touch to our visual impressions of the setting: "It seemed to me the most delicious retreat that the imagination of man could conceive. To hear the wind getting up out at sea, to know that the fog was creeping over the desolate flat outside, and to look at the fire and think that there was no house near but this one, and this one a boat, was like enchantment" (p. 34). In this brief passage, David acknowledges the power of the creative imagination to protect man from sometimes ugly reality (though the child would not have put the idea just this way). Dickens's additive structure for word-paintings succeeds in filling out the visual with its aural and tactile components. Together the various senses dramatize the child's sense of enchanted isolation. Picturesque word-paintings in *David Copperfield* always occur in striking conjunction with words such as "fairy-tale," "enchantment," or "dreamlike." They offer us the reverse of *Barnaby Rudge*'s kinetic word-paintings of nightmare and chaos; and they consistently evoke a magical transformation of ordinary states of vision.

In a recent catalogue of visualizations in the Victorian novel, Michael Irwin comments, "A picturesque redundancy of detail is characteristic of Dickens' descriptions in *David Copperfield*."[9] Such redundancy may appear in the early sections of the novel, such as the word-painting of Peggotty's houseboat that was just discussed. But such descriptive habits give way, once David arrives at Dover, to more symbolic descriptive modes whose details are the very opposite of redundant, for they relate organically to the themes of the novel. I have suggested previously that in contrast to set pieces the most successful word-paintings incorporate some sense of dramatic progress into their visual perspectives. Dickens does this by means of the word-portrait and the verbal tableau.

Of the two kinds of word-paintings, the word-portrait is the more noticeable and more frequent in *David Copperfield*. As was his habit throughout his career, Dickens often introduces a new character into the narrative here with a single paragraph that briefly sketches David's first visual impression of that individual. Dickens's correspondence with his illustrators suggests that he wrote such passages partly to simplify the work of the artists.[10] Certainly, the unusual vigor of Dickens's visual imagination is well documented. Although our first impressions of the less important characters in this novel often quickly condense into caricature (Uriah Heep is perhaps the best example of this tendency) they are introduced with a rather full and accurate visualization of their appearance.

Most of the noteworthy examples of word-portraits in *David Copperfield* occur, as might be expected, in the first third of the novel. Descriptive virtuosity appears in the way Dickens manages to introduce a variety of effects into an essentially repetitive introductory device. Often these word-portraits are used primarily for comic effect. Our first sustained look at Ham, for instance, anticipates the external view of Peggotty's boat in a humorous way. Somehow he fits his house, with its iron funnel chimney and its slightly askew tilt.

> He was now a huge, strong fellow of six feet high, broad in proportion and round-shouldered; but with a simpering boy's face and curly light hair that gave him quite a sheepish look. He was dressed in a canvas jacket, and a pair of such very stiff trousers that they would have stood quite well alone, without any legs in them. And you couldn't so properly have said he wore a hat, as that he was covered in a-top, like an old building, with something pitchy. (pp. 30–31)

The terms of this visual description are clearly distorted for comic and dramatic effect, but the word-portrait also succeeds in showing us Ham's essential nature—his simple dignity and naive integrity—and the way he looks.

The terms of the description of Ham locate this individual among those David loves and admires. Miss Murdstone, on the other hand, clearly comes from a dehumanized, unfeeling world outside the charmed circle of the Peggottys.

> It was Miss Murdstone who was arrived, and a gloomy-looking lady she was; dark, like her brother, whom she greatly resembled in face and voice, and with very heavy eyebrows, nearly meeting over her large nose, as if, being disabled by the wrongs of her sex from wearing whiskers, she had carried them to that account. She brought with her two uncompromising hard black boxes, with her initials on the lids in hard brass nails. When she paid the coachman she took her money out of a hard steel purse, and she kept the purse in a very jail of a bag which hung upon her arm by a heavy chain, and shut up like a bite. I had never, at that time, seen such a metallic lady altogether as Miss Murdstone was. (p. 50)

Who can forget the grim Miss Murdstone? Her word-portrait is internally consistent, and the very opposite of enchantment, closer to the horrific fantasy of the stepsisters in *Cinderella* or the queen in *Snow White*. Repeated adjectives emphasize the qualities of hardness, darkness, and coldness, and David's final comment summarizes the total effect. This single paragraph establishes the context for every subsequent appearance of Miss Murdstone; her role in the novel is that of consistent antagonist to David, both in his relationship with his own mother, and later, Dora. Description—here in the form of word-portraiture—participates fully in the general theme of the conflict between the worlds of the mind and the heart.

In subsequent word-portraits, the adult narrator often comments on his ability to see again the figures from his early days in his imagination. Describing Mr. Peggotty, for example, the narrator remarks, "He stands before me again, his bluff, hairy face irradiating with a joyful love and pride, for which I can find no description" (p. 110). Or, when he is reunited with Miss Betsy at Dover, he must correct his early memories of her with a proper vision. No longer "a discontented fairy" (p. 13). Aunt Betsy is now seen to be "a tall, hard-featured lady, but by no means ill-looking. . . . her features were rather handsome than otherwise, tough, unbending and austere. I particularly noticed that she had a very quick, bright eye" (p. 205). The look in a person's eye is often an indication of the soul in the word-portraits of *David Copperfield,* and offers an important hint of whether he or she will be a friend or enemy to David.

The reader occasionally detects a note of frustration in the narrator's descriptions, as if he cannot entirely bring the past into focus for himself, either because of the limits of language or of his art. But the insistence of the backward look always colors our sense of impressions of David's world. Sometimes the narrator is well satisfied with his ability to picture the past. His evocation of David's experiences at Dover, for instance, moves coherently from the word-portraits of Betsy Trotwood, Mr. Dick, and the serving-girl, Janet—a paragraph for each—to a word-painting of the living room. David, the adult narrator, conjures the past with the assistance of immediate sense impressions, and, suddenly he sees again that which was once all-important for him: a home.

> The room was as neat as Janet or my aunt. As I laid down my pen, a moment since, to think of it, the air from the sea came blowing in again, mixed with the perfume of the flowers; and I saw the old-fashioned furniture brightly rubbed and polished, my aunt's inviolable chair and table by the round green fan in the bow-window, the drugget-covered carpet, the cat, the kettle-holder, the two canaries, the old china, the punch-bowl full of dried rose-leaves, the tall press guarding all sorts of bottles and pots, and wonderfully out of keeping with the rest, my dusty self upon the sofa, taking note of everything. (pp. 205–6)

As we noted in the description of Peggotty's house, this interior is entirely appropriate to its owner and reveals something about her basic nature and values. Everything is clean and in order, arranged to be aesthetically pleasing. Again, items in the room are catalogued and described through the perspective of a now-bedraggled child, though not in as much sensuous detail—because David is exhausted, perhaps?—as we had at Peggotty's, a happier period in the boy's life.

Increasingly, precisely described architectural settings operate as analogues for their owners in *David Copperfield;* and, like fully realized word-paintings, extended descriptions of houses and rooms in this novel integrate increasingly tightly with narration and dramatization. Thus, as Steerforth's fortunes descend, and his mother and Rosa sink into despair, David notices a parallel distintegration of the family mansion. Similarly, David's and Dora's house, much later in the novel, bespeaks the tangle and disarray of their lives of childish irresponsibility together.

One of the most famous of all Dickensian word-portraits occurs in convenient juxtaposition with a brief description of the house of a character being introduced. In this case, Aunt Betsy and David pay a visit on lawyer Wickfield, who is to find David employment as scribe to his former teacher, Dr. Strong. We know nothing as yet about the Wickfields, but the fanciful description of their house gives us several hints concerning our appropriate attitudes toward them. The passage also indicates the increasing care Dickens lavishes on his descriptive writing. As a word-painting, the following passage is quite similar to the picturesque mode of the Maypole Inn description in *Barnaby Rudge.*

> At length we stopped before a very old house bulging out over the road—a house with long low lattice-windows bulging out still further, and beams with carved heads on the ends bulging out too, so that I fancied the whole house was leaning forward, trying to see who was passing on the narrow pavement below. It was quite spotless in its cleanliness. The old-fashioned brass knocker on the low arched door, ornamented with carved garlands of fruit and flowers, twinkled like a star; the two stone steps descending to the door were as white as if they had been covered with fair linen; and all the angles and corners, and carvings and mouldings, and quaint little panes of glass, and quainter little windows, though as old as the hills, were as pure as any snow that ever fell upon the hills. (pp. 230–31)

The house clearly participates in the general fantasy-look of the opening section of *David Copperfield,* in which the emphasis is on picturesque descriptive modes. The imagination of the viewer transforms the real details of architecture through an underlying personification in which the building is compared to a fat, nosey, but benevolent old person. The genesis for this analogy, we are told, is David's lively imagination ("I fancied"). Perhaps we can see why he will be a fine reporter in maturity, however, for as delightful as is his imagination, he can simultaneously give us a clear visual impression of the house in its interesting details (lattice-windows, carved beams, etc.). Having previously "read" the architectural hints for narrative viewpoints of their owners in *David Copperfield,* we are prepared to approve of the Wickfields for their spotless, well-cared-for house and its beautiful embellishing with artful carvings, etc. The narrative itself will take the whole subsequent bulk of the book to achieve the joining of David with Agnes Wickfield; but the alert reader of word-paintings and setting in this novel already knows that such a happy ending must be achieved. Thus, in this case, a seemingly neutral word-painting actually signals narrative developments and the proper judgment for the reader to make of Agnes, the eventual heroine. Description here replaces overt narrative commentary, which would mar the attempt to render a first-person narrative.

Our expectations of harmony between house and tenant suffer a rude shock when it is Uriah Heep—chief villain of the novel—who opens the door. We immediately recognize, from his word-portrait, that he does not belong there, but is an unwelcome intruder. Our introduction to him is an excellent example of how Dickens uses word-portraiture to set the dominant visual motifs for a characterization: "When the pony-chaise stopped at the door, and my eyes were intent upon the house, I saw a cadaverous face appear at a small window on the ground-floor (in a little round tower that formed one side of the house), and quickly disappear" (p. 231). The narrator provides instant suspense with the glimpse of a "cadaverous face." Note, also, the way in which he wishes the reader to visualize exactly how the volumes of the architecture are arranged, and the precise relationships between windows, towers, and walls. Although that information appears within a parenthesis, this sort of reportorial detail brings a Dickens novel to life in our imaginations. Uriah soon emerges from the Wickfield house, a disembodied face at first, followed by a physique clearly intended to be repulsive.

> The low arched door then opened, and the face came out. It was quite as cadaverous as it had looked in the window, though in the grain of it there was that tinge of red which is sometimes to be observed in the skins of red-haired people. It belonged to a red-haired person—a youth of fifteen, as I take it now, but looking much older—whose hair was cropped as close as the closest stubble, who had hardly any eyebrows and no eye-lashes, and eyes of a red brown, so unsheltered and unshaded, that I remember wondering how he went to sleep. He was high-shouldered and bony; dressed in decent black, with a white wisp of a neckcloth; buttoned up to the throat; and had a long, lank, skeleton hand, which particularly attracted

my attention, as he stood at the pony's head, rubbing his chin with it, and looking up at us in the chaise. (p. 231)

The scene has the ring of dramatic truth, for we can vividly imagine David, looking down at this strange individual and surveying him from head to foot. This organizes the details of the word-portrait, giving us David's physical and psychological perspective on Uriah. The description, of course, is heavily skewed to reflect David's immediate dislike of the man-boy, for our first view of him is anything but charming. First framed by the window of the house, Uriah now stands below David in the street, in utter opposition to the picturesque details of the house. His sepulchral boniness and hairlessness make us wonder if he might be a fit companion to Miss Murdstone with her hard, metallic nature. Like her, he comes from the world of business—the city—and carries the negative values Dickens associates with these locations at this point in his writing career. David immediately dislikes and fears Uriah.

Before we can forget Uriah's "skeleton hand," the narrator reinforces our first impression with significant repetitions of this feature. At the end of this episode, David, feeling very happy about his new job, generously extends his hand to Uriah in farewell (also in an attempt to overcome his strong aversion to this character): "As I came back I saw Uriah Heep shutting up the office, and feeling friendly towards everybody, went in and spoke to him, and at parting gave him my hand. But oh, what a clammy hand his was! as ghostly to the touch as to the sight! I rubbed mine afterwards to warm it, *and to rub his off*" (p. 237—Dickens's italics). Here, in an extension of Dickens's characteristic technique of reiterating significant details in word-portraits, he augments a brief sketch of a character's appearance with a vivid vignette—in this case, shaking hands with the "cadaver"—to indicate a motif in Uriah's characterization.

In addition, Dickens's verbal tags for characters like Uriah amplify the visual with the aural. Dickens usually develops word-paintings fully by adding aural and, sometimes, tactile and olfactory dimensions. Just as the word-painting of the Maypole expanded to describe sounds and smells, so the brief word-portraits in Dickens are often accompanied by hearing what a character typically says.

Uriah's verbal tag rings variations on "I'm a very umble person" (p. 246). This sentiment recurs so often that it eventually stands for Heep himself, and his most salient qualities, unctiousness and hypocrisy. Posture often augments speech in this case, for he is usually depicted in an obsequious pose. The word-portraits of Rosa Dartle (p. 306) and Miss Mowcher (p. 343) stand out in this novel as other examples of how well Dickens could adapt word-portraits to express the physical and psychological essence of a person. Rosa's scar and Miss Mowcher's enormous head and ogling eyes come to symbolize each of their world views.

The opening descriptions of the Maypole in *Barnaby Rudge* exemplify how Dickens stopped the narrative for long periods of time in order to fill in the background through word-paintings of landscape settings. Now, in *David Copperfield,* this feature of the prose has been replaced by much briefer passages of description, both of setting and character, in the form of word-portraits that show how the world appears to a young boy. By referring often to an important physical attribute, such as Uriah's boney hand or Miss Murdstone's steely demeanor, word-portraits contribute to our sense of character development. At the same time, frequent repetitions of visual and aural quirks often concentrate the introductory portrait, reducing visual appearance to caricature and speech to verbal tag.

By transferring the subject of most composed scenes from landscape to word-portraits and verbal tableaux, Dickens seems to have been following his natural preference for describing people rather than settings. Jerome Buckley argued that Dickens differs from the Romantics because

> his descriptive passages seldom resorted to the "view-hunting" of which Carlyle had accused the Romantic poets; for Charles Dickens felt no response to tranquil or tempestuous nature; he focused his vision on the teeming city, the glooming alleys and draped interiors, the fog blurring ancient stone, the bright costumes silhouetted against town walls—the whole crowded life of London in all its man-made detail.[11]

Although Dickens often includes extended landscape descriptions in *Barnaby Rudge,* there are only two in *David Copperfield.* One occurs in the climactic storm scene in which Ham drowns in a vain attempt to rescue Steerforth, the man who has seduced Ham's beloved, Emily. The other example of the traditional sublime—the only passage of real "scene-hunting"—occurs as prelude to the climax in the narrative of David's education. Since the descriptive technique here is almost exactly like the sublime landscape descriptions of Ann Radcliffe, whose prose we have examined previously, I shall forego a close examination of these passages in favor of discussion of innovations in the basic feature of word-painting. However, a comment is necessary concerning the consistency of placement of these two picturesque descriptions relative to their narrative in *David Copperfield.* In each case, the description occurs at a climactic point in the story. David's Alpine revelation is central to the conventional theme of the *bildungsroman,* the journey of the hero toward maturity. As David sits looking out at the Alps—weeping over Nature's serene beauty at sunset and the letter he has just received from Agnes—he finally recognizes what has been apparent, at least to the reader, for some time. Agnes has always loved him selflessly; and, finally, three years after his self-imposed exile, he recognizes that he returns her love. This revelation frees him from the past, and he can return to England at last. Thus, a traditional, though sentimentalized, example of the sublime serves as catalyst for revelation and denouement. The passage does not have the vitality and originality of Dickens's word-portraits and verbal tableaux in *David Copperfield,* however, and represents a flagging of Dickens's visual sense. It seems merely formulaic.

The extended storm description, on the other hand, though sublime, obviously excites Dickens more. It stops short of being an objective correlative for David's strong emotions, but the description succeeds in bringing the story of Ham, Emily, and Steerforth to a dramatic conclusion. Throughout the storm, the reader stays securely anchored to David's point of view, and there are no long passages of kinetic visualizations of the scene such as we had in *Barnaby Rudge*. Raw nature interests the narrator less than its effects on the protagonist. Here again, then, we see descriptive materials both dramatized and absorbed by the emphasis on character and narrative developments.

A brief discussion of the second interesting new emphasis in subject and form for word-paintings concludes our examination of the visually oriented descriptive modes of *David Copperfield*. In a suggestive study of the Victorian illustrations of Dickens's novels, John Harvey notes, "The chief feature of the *Copperfield* illustrations is the greatly extended use of the 'tableau.' "[12] Harvey summarizes Dickens's descriptive method at such junctures as follows:

> In (*David Copperfield*) Dickens will momentarily arrest his characters in a significant grouping which he describes as a 'picture' and which is evidently conceived with an illustration in mind. This pictorial technique had not occurred to Dickens at the start of the novel: in the first number a significant moment of this kind comes (Harvey is referring to Emily on the jetty), and Dickens explicitly asserts his pictorial qualities, but there is no illustration. . . . (p. 142)

Harvey corroborates our argument that Dickens's prose is increasingly amenable to the tableau style of illustration, but Harvey considers only those scenes that were actually illustrated. He does not note the shift in emphasis from word-paintings to word-portraits and verbal tableaux that we have been tracing in the works of Dickens, nor does he connect new habits of vision with changes in David's perspective as he matures.

Another recent critic concerned with the tableau style of illustration in Victorian visual arts offers us a further definition of that style. Writing about Cruikshank's illustrations for Ainsworth's novels, Jonathan Hill tells us that a tableau style of illustration "depicts moments of narrative climax in framed static compositions" (p. 430). This style, derived from the "widely used theatrical device of . . . the dramatic 'tableau vivant,' " so popular on the London stage in the 1830s, had the following compositional characteristics: it replaced agitated movement between figures with static patterning which was reinforced by firm outlines, close-ups of the figures, an enclosed space, dramatic high-contrast tones, and a very heavily accentuated frame (p. 435). Of course Hill's scheme refers to a style of illustration, but if, as Harvey argues, Dickens were writing with a possible tableau illustration in mind, we might expect some of these visual features to be evident in the prose. It is my contention that selected scenes—especially the treatment of the Annie-Doctor Strong-Jack Maldon drama—offer a strong verbal analogue to the tableau vivant as defined here.

Hill tells us, further, that Dickens's novels as early as *Pickwick* were often dramatized on stage as tableaux vivants based on the novel's illustrations (p. 441). Dickens might well have been drawn to this "widespread theatrical tendency toward pictorialism" (p. 442), not only because his own novels were the subject of such stage treatment, but also because, with his love of theatricality and his unusually vivid visual imagination, he would quickly have seized on the possibilities of such a technique to focus the narrative climaxes of his own stories.

But how does this popular stage form of entertainment permeate the verbal style of Dickens's descriptive passages in *David Copperfield?* The frozen poses of figures (who are often depicted not speaking) at key moments in the narrative, the framing of these figures by a door or window opening on a small enclosed interior space, and the fact that the scene is viewed from the single perspective of one observer all characterize the verbal tableaux in *David Copperfield*. Often such scenes occur at the ends of chapters, though they sometimes introduce a dramatic episode. And all the important verbal tableaux in this novel center on a woman who is important to David at a certain stage of his development. If we think back over the novel, we remember David's young mother bending over her child; we recall Emily poised on the brink of an abyss; we think of Peggotty as he remembers her when he returns to the houseboat after a long absence, accompanied by Steerforth; and we visualize Annie Strong, whose enigmatic passion clearly both fascinates and terrifies David.

Visually oriented frozen moments often occur in *David Copperfield,* as Harvey notes, to fill a momentary pause in the action, or to allow the adult narrator, looking back over his life, to organize his memories, to recognize the perfection of a moment, and to try to keep it forever. For instance, when David returns home to his mother for the last time, and finds her nursing the baby brother he is soon to lose along with her, the frozen tableau signifies his longing to stop time. Although the mature narrator knows that it is impossible to escape time, the impetus for the verbal tableau derives from the adult narrator's desire to make his imagination overcome time, to fix the inchoate materials of his childhood in the matrix of art.

No small part of the effectiveness of the verbal tableaux in *David Copperfield* rises from the peculiar intensity of their visualization. This quality comes, of course, from the emotions of the observer. In most cases, David himself composes these tableaux vivants, as we are told in the text, often describing them as "pictures." Hill tells us that the dramatic tableaux vivants on the Victorian stage were "sometimes referred to by the contemporary synonyms 'picture' or 'group'" (p. 437), a fact that would explain another source for so naming these visual scenes.

In most cases the verbal tableaux in our text occur either as David returns to loved ones from a long separation (the scenes with his mother and Peggotty), or when he intrudes upon a dramatic scene already in progress between people about whom he cares deeply. In both instances, the scene is preternaturally sharp because so abruptly perceived and so isolated from normal occurrences. Usually such scenes jump from the page as David moves alone from a dark place into a lighted room full of people. David composes these verbal pictures as he did the picturesque ones, but the emotion, more immediate and strong, seems to spill over into the surrounding story. Dickens accomplishes this effect by constantly referring back to the vivid scene, or by commenting at the time on what that scene will mean to the future. Foreshadowing characteristically accompanies Dickens's verbal tableaux. Though they are framed and distanced from the observer, David, by door or window frame, the visual and emotional intensity of these scenes conveys a sense of their importance as climactic moments in the development of the protagonist and of the narrative of his life.

The narrator gives us verbal tableaux of Emily and of Annie Strong that demonstrate how this technique sets up iconographic motifs for each that remain constant through the novel. The pictorialization of each woman expresses an essential truth of her nature in visual terms. For Emily, life is a perilous journey, and her impetuous nature puts her often at the edge of disaster. Our first "picture" of Emily establishes this iconographic motif. As David, her childhood playmate, watches in terror for her safety, she dares to walk a high plank.

> She started from my side, and ran along a jagged timber which protruded from the place we stood upon, and overhung the deep water at some height, without the least defence. The incident is so impressed on my remembrance, that if I were a draughtsman I could draw its form here, I dare say, accurately as it was that day, and little Em'ly springing forward to her destruction (as it appeared to me), with a look that I have never forgotten, directed far out to sea. (p. 38)

The drama of the physical situation, the helplessness of the observer, and the wild expression in Emily's eyes would be enough to impress the scene upon the reader. But the narrator reinforces this frozen moment with characteristic narrative foreshadowing, to be sure that we see how significant this moment really is.

> There has been a time since—I do not say it lasted long, but it has been—when I have asked myself the question, would it have been better for little Em'ly to have had the waters close above her head that morning in my sight; and when I have answered Yes.
> This may be premature. I have set it down too soon, perhaps. But let it stand. (p. 39)

Emily's intrinsically reckless nature is evident in this dramatic scene, and helps explain her rash elopement with Steerforth. But the scene is heavily overlaid with the point of view of the adult narrator, who reminds us of his pictorial imagination, and in his concluding remarks, shows his regret at the loss of chronology. But significantly, he does not remove the "premature" suggestion; of course, it is intended to create suspense and continuity in the narrative.

Later, when David and Steerforth intrude upon the scene of Emily's betrothal to Ham, we again catch Emily, in another verbal tableau, frozen in the act of springing again (though this time, to safety): "little Em'ly herself, blushing and shy, but delighted with Mr. Peggotty's delight, as her joyful eyes expressed, was stopped by our entrance (for she saw us first) in the very act of springing from Ham to nestle in Mr. Peggotty's embrace" (p. 328). This moment is another in the series of verbal tableaux of Emily, and resonates in the narrator's mind because it is the last time the Peggottys will compose a happy family group. Thus we note the way in which verbal tableaux often constitute the very apexes of the narrative in *David Copperfield* and serve as emphasis for moments of climax.

The other major cluster of verbal tableaux that will concern us here dramatizes the Annie-Doctor Strong-Jack Maldon subplot. No less than four times—widely separated in the narrative—does Dickens stop the action to construct a recurrent scene in which Doctor Strong's beautiful young wife, Annie, kneels before her husband in a suppliant pose. Feminists could make much of Dickens's fondness for such iconography in the novel; certainly the four scenes possess a disquieting emotional tone, unaccounted for even by David's perspective on these scenes and his attempt to avoid acknowledging their reflection on his own marriage to Dora. Like Emily's, Annie's story, too, at first appears to be one of betrayal and seduction, two situations Dickens the writer was notoriously unable to handle effectively in his prose. The verbal tableaux involving Annie, with their recurrent iconographic motifs, suggest powerful and mysterious forces at work in the relationship between Annie, her husband, and the scoundrel Jack Maldon, who clearly has no good intentions toward either of them.

David's first sight of Annie sets the visual motif for her subsequent appearances in the novel. When he is first introduced to his new employer, he sees Annie, also: "Sitting at work, not far off from Doctor Strong, was a very pretty young lady—whom he called Annie, and who was his daughter, I supposed—who got me out of my difficulty by kneeling down to put Doctor Strong's shoes on, and button his gaiters, which she did with great cheerfulness and quickness" (p. 238). While this brief picture might not have impressed the reader, the pose soon recurs, and seizes our attention, as it does David's. Passing one night from the dark, deserted supper-room to the Doctor's study in search of a candle, he stumbles upon a brightly illuminated scene: "The Doctor was sitting in his easy-chair by the fireside, and his young wife was on a stool by his feet" (p. 260). To this striking pose, the narrator adds the dramatic expression on Annie's beautiful face; it is this that fixes his attention.

The Doctor, with a complacent smile, was reading aloud some manuscript explanation or statement of a theory out of that interminable Dictionary, and she was looking up at him, but with such a face as I never saw—it was so beautiful in its form, it was so ashy pale, it was so fixed in its abstraction, it was so full of a wild, sleep-walking dreamy horror of

> I don't know what. The eyes were wide open, and her brown hair fell in two rich clusters on her shoulders, and on her white dress, disordered by the want of the lost ribbon. Distinctly as I recollect her look, I cannot say of what it was expressive. I cannot even say of what it is expressive to me now. . . . (p. 260)

David speculates on what her look might be: penitent, humble, ashamed, loving, trustful. His comments insistently remind us of his presence in the room and the way in which he sees such scenes "rise again" in his memory. The sensuality of the lovely draped female figure and the contrast between her subservient pose and the desperate, passionate look in her eyes heightens the suspense associated with her situation, and disturbs the viewer.

David's entrance interrupts and dissolves the tableau, but the way Annie speaks—"in a rapid, urgent manner"—requesting to be allowed to stay with her husband that evening, impresses David with the mood of the moment even more.

> And as she turned again towards him, after glancing at me as I left the room and went out at the door, I saw her cross her hands upon his knee, and look up at him with the same face, something quieted, as he resumed his reading.
>
>   It made a great impression on me, and I remembered it a long time afterwards, as I shall have occasion to narrate when the time comes. (p. 260)

The time to which the narrator refers here, at the end of chapter 16, does not arrive until four hundred and thirty pages later, and the reader would be forgiven for forgetting this particular scene. But Dickens uses similar iconography in recurrent verbal tableaux both to remind us of the story of Annie and Doctor Strong and to lend coherence to his narrative, when he finally relieves the suspense that has accompanied Annie's appearances through the novel. The descriptive method insures narrative coherence when he again poses Annie in a kneeling position and his other characters in poses that echo their earlier composition. The scene, in which David, Aunt Betsy, and Mr. Dick gather to help Annie and Dr. Strong work out their misunderstanding reminds the reader of a stage play, where all the important characters come on stage for the denouement. And here we have an excellent example of how word-painting—now in the more dramatic form of the verbal tableau—is used to convey a climactic moment in the narrative.

Here, at last, we have an extended visually oriented description to set beside the sublime word-paintings of landscape in Radcliffe's novels and the kinetic word-paintings of mob action in Dickens's *Barnaby Rudge*. In it, we see how Dickens manages to saturate his verbal tableaux with narrative and dramatic significance. The scene reminds us of melodrama, with its frozen, exaggerated poses and gestures:

> But who got first into the study, or how Mrs. Markleham settled herself in a moment in her easy-chair, or how my aunt and I came to be left together near the door . . . I have forgotten,

if I ever knew. But this I know—that we saw the Doctor before he saw us, sitting at his table, among the folio volumes in which he delighted, resting his head calmly on his hand. That, in the same moment, we saw Mrs. Strong glide in, pale and trembling. That Mr. Dick supported her on his arm. That he laid his other hand upon the Doctor's arm, causing him to look up with an abstracted air. That, as the Doctor moved his head, his wife dropped down on one knee at his feet, and, with her hands imploringly lifted, fixed upon his face the memorable look I have never forgotten. That at this sight Mrs. Markleham dropped the newspaper, and stared more than like a figurehead intended for a ship to be called The Astonishment, than anything else I can think of. (pp. 691–92)

This frozen moment soon gives way to a long, sentimental scene in which Annie removes the cloud of suspicion from her relationship with Doctor Strong in a series of speeches dripping with pathos. But before the tableau dissolves, let us note how well it adheres to Hill's definition of the tableau vivant on the Victorian stage. The figures are precisely placed in a small, enclosed room in poses characteristic of each. Annie, again kneeling before her husband, is this time raised by Mr. Dick as perfect trust is restored between man and wife. To assure that we connect this scene with the earlier verbal tableau, Annie speaks of that previous moment "when I came to you that night to lay down all my load of shame and grief" (p. 698). Static patterning replaces the agitated movement of the figures, and they are frozen in dramatic gestures close enough to be able to see the look in Annie's eyes. The frame, of course, is the room itself, and also the context into which David puts this scene relative to his own life. Iconography prefigures meaning here, in contrast to the less programmatic scenes of mobs and disorder in *Barnaby Rudge*.

The scene ends with David reflecting on the inadequacies of his own marriage and his "undisciplined heart." Juxtaposition of David's with Annie's marriage does the work of narrative commentary indirectly. And verbal tableaux have extended the uses of word-paintings to narrative.

Little Dorrit: The Visual as Symbolic Subtext to Narration

Thus far the present study demonstrates Dickens's decreasing use of extended picturesque word-paintings and his increasing reliance on the word-portrait and the verbal tableau to convey climactic points in the narrative. This development in Dickens's descriptive technique yields an increasing coherence among descriptive, narrative, and dramatic materials in novels of this writer's middle and later period, because the three modes now relate organically to important themes and the development of characters.

Now I intend to demonstrate how Dickens sometimes symbolically prefigures changes in sensibilities of characters in the imagery and form of late word-paintings in *Little Dorrit*. In this novel, he moves progressively toward more symbolic word-paintings and more sophisticated descriptive writing in general. I shall show this by an examination of the central symbolic metaphor in *Little Dorrit*, the opposition between sunlight and shadow. Dickens's monthly plans for *Little Dorrit* inform us that he thought of the major visual motif—sunlight and shadow—as a rather stark and simplistic reiteration of the contrast between light and dark. J. Hillis Miller notes that "a greater symbolic unity of conception" than hitherto evident in his work characterizes all three of Dickens's great, dark novels of his middle period—*Bleak House, Little Dorrit,* and *Our Mutual Friend*.[13] But *Little Dorrit* is especially interesting for the ways in which Dickens depends constantly and explicitly on his dominant symbol from the title of the novel's first chapter to its concluding sentence. In addition, the author's evolving sense of the central experiences in the novel creates a changing imagery that seriously undercuts the optimistic surface meaning of its conclusion. Thus, attention to a recurrent visual element in *Little Dorrit* signals important changes in the sensibilities of either the main characters or the narrator. In so relating, word-painting and other visually oriented imagery sequences assume an even more intimate relationship with narrative than has been the case in most previous Dickens novels.

Study of the major recurrent iconographic motif in *Little Dorrit* also illuminates Dickens's particular cast of imagination in the mid-1850s, when we sense that Dickens subtly altered the imagery to conform with his growing loss of confidence both in the simpler solutions of his earlier period, and in the power of love to solve human problems. I shall examine the ways in which the metaphor of sunlight and shade serves as stylistic foundation, as expression of theme, and as foundation for structure in *Little Dorrit,* sometimes supporting, other times subverting textual intentions.

In chapter 1 the central image of sunlight and shadow begins as physical description (here are located the more traditional word-paintings of setting), gradually modulating its meanings and internalizing within characters and setting alike until it simultaneously expresses the theme of the novel: imprisonment by self and society.

Those who would accuse Dickens of an overly conventional treatment of light and dark in this novel have failed to see how subtly this motif shapes the entire narrative. One is easily fooled by the disarming openness of the narrator, who appears to present all the essential aspects of the meaning for sunlight and shadow at the beginning of the novel. Yet, by paying close attention, the alert reader notes the gradual shifts in the meaning of the shadow image until its ultimate reversal of the traditional associations with darkness, evil, and defeat.

At the beginning of the novel, however, the explicit meanings of sunlight and shadow indicate that Dickens works in an entirely different mode from symbolists who gradually deepen the ambiguity of their symbols which fuse with structure, character, and theme. In Dickens's *Little Dorrit*, the major early additive effect is accomplished by assembling analogous images. A consistent set of attributes and ideas almost always accompanies the sunlight/shade figure, revealing the artist's imaginative association with this image. The motif of sunlight and shadow usually associates with dirt and dust, contagion and disease, ambiguous guilty secrets from the past, joylessness and lack of will, and the journey and labyrinth motifs.[14] These recur with monotonous and deliberative effect, especially throughout Book One.

The artistic imagination at work in *Little Dorrit* soon demonstrates difficulty with holding both sides of the contrasting figure of sunlight and shadow in balance after the early chapters of the novel. Although *Little Dorrit* begins with a careful opposing of sunlight and shade, we quickly move into a dark, wet, gloomy world with Arthur Clennam's return to England, locus of physical and psychological prisons in this novel. Dickens suppresses the sunlight aspect of the figure throughout Book One, concentrating instead on an intensification of his dark vision of man and society. For example, he avoids a description of Little Dorrit's childhood forays into the countryside with the turnkey, although clearly, these journeys are the high point of her childhood. The excursions are dismissed in a single sentence. Later, the author maintains the atmosphere of gloom by focusing, not on the beauties of the countryside, but on Arthur's melancholic internal state as he leaves London for a visit to the Meagleses. Although their country home represents country joys and the warmth of family life, the reader hears only of Arthur's unhappiness and frustration in his unrequited and secret love for Pet.

But as the narrative advances into Book Two, it would seem that Dickens is increasingly uncomfortable with the ramifications of such a pessimistic vision of man's possibilities for self-fulfillment, and he begins to manipulate the meanings of his dominant motifs more and more obviously. There is a significant decrease in references to the shadow image until halfway through the second Book, where they suddenly and dramatically resurface in the story of William Dorrit's pathetic self-exposure and death. Also, images of divine and natural light in combination with darkness begin to build toward the denouement in the last quarter of the novel, undercutting the pessimism of the implied world view, but never entirely obliterating it.

Although Arthur and Little Dorrit marry at the end of the novel and emerge from the darkness of the Marshalsea into the bright light of the marketplace, the thrust of the imagery indicates a somewhat less than joyful resolution. While it is almost too painfully clear that Dickens means to present light conquering darkness, the working out of the sunlight/shade motif creates an increasingly twilight effect, as the two elements mix in the last quarter of the novel. This development in the primary symbolic motif undercuts and diminishes the final marriage scene, suggesting that the protagonists will experience only a muted joy, always mixed with sadness—the result of their lost years and blighted hopes. One concludes *Little Dorrit* with the feeling that the shadow element has proven too strong for the opposing sunlight on the deepest levels of meaning.

The twilight modulation represents one important aspect of the dominant motif that is not expressed at the very beginning of the novel. And twilight turns out to be a telling image for the real world view of *Little Dorrit*. In fact, Dickens is saying, things in this world are not clear and unalloyed: truth exists in some murky twilight condition, and people are trapped because they cannot see their way clearly. It is extremely interesting that this image seems to hold appeal for other major mid- and late-Victorian writers besides Dickens—writers such as Tennyson, Rossetti, and Swinburne. All these writers seem attracted to transitional moments between one state of being and another, where the situation is uncertain but full of possibility. The last quarter of *Little Dorrit* demonstrates Dickens's attraction to this transitional state.

The shadow gradually covers and unifies all the elements in the vast canvas of *Little Dorrit*—from the highest social representatives, the Merdles, to the lowest, the tenants of the Marshalsea—in a chiaroscuro effect that links the external with the internal prisons of this novel. The movement of the imagery supports the impression that Charles Dickens is being forced, in this middle period of his great novels, to confront the personal discomfort of paradox and irrationality. The working title for *Little Dorrit* points to this essential theme: "Nobody's Fault." The sufferings and disasters in this novel, are, in the widest sense, nobody's fault because they are everybody's fault. Man has allowed society to construct irrational structures of oppression symbolized here by the Marshalsea and the Circumlocution Office. Both are vast and uncontrollable bureaucracies that destroy individual freedom, yet were created by well-intentioned men who had originally hoped to bring order and justice to society's governing structures.

Conversely, the pervasive structural use of coincidence and chance in the plotting of *Little Dorrit* would seem to imply a rational universe where everything and everyone ultimately interrelate in a comprehensible pattern. The motifs of the labyrinth and the journey of life would seem to support such a theme. And yet, the darkness that lies over all the elements in this novel indicates that man is unable to see his direction or goal. Thus, rational and irrational tendencies seem to war against each other. This helps explain both the conceptual difficulties of *Little Dorrit* and the curiously unconvincing effect of the work's happy ending.

This ending presents the mixed nature of the real world that awaits Arthur and Little Dorrit. Although they have been saved through the healing power of mutual love, the troubled, dark world does not change: "They went quietly down into the roaring streets, inseparable and blessed; and as they passed along in sunlight and shade, the noisy and the eager, and the arrogant and the froward and the vain, fretted and chafed, and made their usual uproar"[15] (p. 895). Sunlight and shade—now fused in the story of Arthur and Little Dorrit—remain central to the expression of the book's meaning and signal the cancelling of our ordinary associations between darkness, descent, defeat, and death. Although the protagonists, much chastened by life, have now achieved a mellow acceptance of both sunlight and shadow as part of the world's realities, the final note reminds us of the chaos of life and the illusory nature of free will. A rational world view must be abandoned for the murkier and much more unsettling truths of a world in which the way things are is, increasingly, "Nobody's Fault." One sees a modern state of generalized anxiety and guilt reflected in the movement of the dominant motifs of *Little Dorrit:* the dark journey of life, the bewildering labyrinth, as, over both these and the novel itself, the shadow falls.

The discussion so far summarizes the general movement of the sunlight and shadow motif in *Little Dorrit*. I will now investigate how its use and transmogrification in key scenes of the novel demonstrate its centrality to the structure and meaning of the work. Such examination supports Edmund Wilson's contention that "Charles Dickens' symbolism is of a more complicated reference and a deeper implication than metaphors that hang as emblems over the door."[16] Such a discussion will also illustrate Praz's designation of *Little Dorrit*'s tone as a work in which "a positively revolutionary tone is achieved . . . through the mixed nature of riches and vice, poverty and virtue."[17] Truth itself assumes a revolutionary tone of ambiguity which is supported by the mixing of darkness with light, the major image pattern in this novel.

Little Dorrit opens with a fascinating word picture of Marseilles, "burning in the sun" in late August, and introduces virtually all the major themes and symbolic motifs in four short paragraphs. The title of this opening chapter, "Sunlight and Shade" (also recorded as the initial phrase in Dickens's monthly number plans for the section), signals the stylistic and structural primacy of this figure. The description moves from the bright, parched landscape, to the foul harbor waters, to the dusty roads (the journey motif begins here), to the twilight world of the churches. The churches offer relief from the "fiery river" of heat and unpleasant brightness, but they also contain nightmarish figures, "dreamily peopled with ugly old shadows piously dozing, spitting, and begging" (p. 40). Thus, darkness immediately associates with dreaming and nightmare, with shadow, dust, and foul odors, with menacing secret things, and with religion as an ambivalent, problematical refuge. The effect of the extreme brightness next to the dark, shadowy churches is like some hallucinatory or surrealistic dream, heightened by the apocalyptic echoes of the city burning. Light and shade are physical entities, first, in *Little Dorrit*, but the intensity of the wasteland description of Marseilles renders a feeling of ominous events that will be an important aspect of the overall mood of this novel.

Along with an emphasis on light's destructive (burning) quality, the opening description immediately associates light with vision, a traditional metaphor for intellectual, emotional, or religious insight. Yet the religious echoes for the sunlight/shadow motif seem, from the first, neither seriously intended nor systematically worked out. Mrs. Clennam is obviously the vehicle for the artist's comments on a repressive Puritanism; she is associated throughout the novel with darkness and crippling secrets from the past. Little Dorrit, on the other hand, is increasingly associated with light as the book nears its conclusion, but she is the agent of the natural light of love rather than the light of religious conversion. These echoes play in the background of the motif, but do not seem to comprise its major associations.

This novel primarily concerns itself with the development of emotional, rather than intellectual or religious, insight in Arthur Clennam and other characters. The theme begins with the first paragraph of the book. The reader is immediately confronted with the staring of strangers, eyes, houses, walls, streets, roads, and hills, in Dickens's typically animistic manner. Yet the rhetoric deepens at once to express an internal state. "The universal stare made the eyes ache." Here the reference is to the sense of vision as painful and hard to bear. Characters in the novel, from the Dorrits to the Barnacles, seem most comfortable in the softened light of shaded windows in the prisons of their lives. The ones capable of realizing how things really are often do so only when imprisoned. Arthur recognizes his love for Little Dorrit, and its reciprocation, only when he is finally himself incarcerated. She has always known the truth of her feelings, perhaps because most of her life has been spent in jail.

The association between physical and psychological discomfort and light is set up in the opening paragraphs of the novel. The thick texture of dust, burning heat, unrelenting brightness, stagnation and aridity quickly transfers its oppressive qualities to a contrasting, still more claustrophobic place, the "villainous prison" of Marseilles. Here, light is reflected, barred, tainted, and the darkness intensifies the discomfort. While Marseilles is only incidentally important as setting, it initiates the theme of the contagion of imprisonment, and the idea of the world itself as one vast, inescapable jail.

The ascent of the turnkey and his little blond daughter up the narrow, dark, winding stair to the cell of Rigaud and St. John Cavalletto introduces the wanderer or seeker motif in the novel that feeds into the symbolic metaphor of life as a weary, arduous journey. The child, her face "touched with divine compassion," is a surrogate for the role Little Dorrit will play in the lives of her father and Arthur. A structuralist myth of the loved one leading the beloved from darkness to light fuses the shadow motif of the journey of life with echoes of the Orphic myth that resonate beneath the surface of this and other mid-century Victorian works (Rossetti's *The House of Life* is another). In the case of Arthur's and Little Dorrit's love story, significant reversals of the classical myth occur, for it is the woman who takes on the Orphic role, ascending the narrow stair to the dark place to retrieve the beloved. But, where Orpheus lost Eurydice when he looked back at her in the twilight, here the woman leads the man downward from the darkness of the Marshalsea to the light of the marketplace, and succeeds, though not a poet, where Orpheus failed.

Associations between Little Dorrit as the source of light, and the end of Arthur's long, dark pilgrimage surface and resolve themselves at two important junctures of their love story. The first of these occurs early on, as Arthur sits dreaming before a dying fire, his thoughts sinking downward towards death. As he reviews his past, the narrator notes that, "leaving himself in the dark, it (his disappointed mind) could rise into the light, seeing it shine on others and hailing it" (p. 206). As he sadly considers his lack of "any staff to bear him company upon his downward journey" (note the echoes of *Pilgrim's Progress* here), the door softly opens to reveal that which he has found at the end of his life's sad journey: Little Dorrit. It is clear that she is to reverse his descent to death, and to restore his drooping spirits with the restoratives of natural healthiness and love.

Another visual analogue signals that the pattern of descent will soon reverse late in the book as Arthur sits, again languishing in darkness, a prisoner in the Marshalsea:

> Looking back upon his own poor story, she was its vanishing-point. Everything in its perspective led to her innocent figure. He had travelled thousands of miles towards it; previous unquiet hopes and doubts had worked themselves out before it; it was the centre of the interest of his life; it was the termination of everything that was good and pleasant in it; beyond, there was nothing but mere waste and darkened sky. (pp. 801–2)

This moment of vision crystalizes and anticipates the novel's denouement. On a superficial level, Little Dorrit, the object of Arthur's quest, serves as source of his vision. But, on a symbolic level, the pervasiveness of the shadow vitiates this final fulfillment, for the murky darkness can overcome the spots of light Little Dorrit provides.

With the release of the Dorrits from the Marshalsea at the conclusion of Book One, the shadow motif is suppressed only to return in another mode, as the theme of man's internal psychological prisons gains ascendancy in the plot. Book Two, "Riches," presents obvious parallels to Book One, "Poverty." Again we encounter, at the outset, a group of weary travellers moving through another bright landscape, this time the frozen wasteland of the Swiss Alps in winter. But the brightness still hurts "unaccustomed eyes" (p. 483), and the wasteland of frigidity, barrenness, and desolation presents an even more ominous and perilous site than Marseilles had been. As darkness and night approach, the travellers seek refuge in the monastery of St. Bernard. This location is a prison with a difference: this time, it is the travellers themselves who create their own internal prisons through the secret identities each wishes to suppress. We recognize the Dorrits and Rigaud at once. And, as the narrator makes all too clear, while the "pilgrims" seek "a new existence," such a possibility is only a "delusion" (p. 504). Little Dorrit suffers increasingly from her loss of identity and sense of place. She tells Arthur that the real world, with all its beauties, seems but a dream, and only the Marshalsea "reality" for her. Thus, once again, we are presented with the theme that we carry our own inescapable internal prisons within us.

Gradually, and inexorably, the shadow of the Marshalsea returns, particularly emphatically at climactic moments in Book Two, but increasingly fused with images of light to create that peculiar twilight effect noted previously. The shadow chills us with its penetration to the very soul of Little Dorrit's father, William; it finally resurfaces in the narrative in his horrifying and pathetic public breakdown in the midst of the high society to which he aspires. Once he reverts to the cringing beggar, the Father of the Marshalsea stands exposed once again and the imposter is destroyed.

Yet, just at the narrative's most pessimistic moment, when the inescapability of the internal prison of the self stands most starkly exposed, Dickens begins to sound those gathering notes of divine and natural light to which we have been referring. While the shadow of the Marshalsea mutates into the shadow of death, the same cosmic perspective used at the conclusion of so many early chapters in the book draws our attention from the pathos of William's wasted life toward the first full articulation of the lyrical beauties of the natural world:

> It was a moonlight night; but the moon rose late, being long past the full. When it was high in the peaceful firmament, it shone through half-closed lattice blinds in the solemn room where the stumblings and wanderings of a life had so lately ended. . . . The two brothers were before their Father; far beyond the twilight judgment of this world; high above its mists and obscurities. (pp. 713–15)

Death and the shadow here assume those qualities of peace, repose, and transcendance for which Little Dorrit and Arthur also yearn at moments of stress in their lives. The narrator's compassionate tone and Biblical language soften the harsh statement of the world view implied above: that man's vision must be misty and obscure in the twilight of this life.

The working out of the relationship between Arthur and Little Dorrit comprises the subject of the last quarter of the novel. The end of their long separation is accompanied by the last major development of the shadow motif. This new meaning dramatically deepens the ambiguity and richness of the motif of sunlight and shade and supports the contention that Dickens's use of symbols is both subtler and more skillful than would seem to be the case upon a superficial reading of *Little Dorrit*. The reunion of Arthur and Little Dorrit within the walls of the Marshalsea is accompanied by the transformation of the shadow from a negative to a positive symbol.

Arthur has finally succumbed to the Marshalsea, where he sits, again dozing and dreaming, disoriented and lacking will, sinking toward psychological and physical death. Little Dorrit returns to him, bringing with her triumphant fertility, healthiness, and hope symbolized by her gift of spring flowers. Though dressed in black, "her tears dropping on him as the rain from Heaven," she is "angelically comforting and true" (p. 825). The prison at last becomes a refuge from an antipathetic world, and the shadow, now protecting and nurturing their love, "fell like light upon him" (p. 827). But the light is mixed with the residue of darkness which will remind us of the dark world outside that tinctures the happiness of the lovers.

Actually, the transformation of the sunlight/shadow motif has been anticipated by the strange and important fairy tale Little Dorrit tells Maggy earlier in the narrative. By recalling this tale at the climactic moment of reunion in the Marshalsea, Dickens underlines its centrality for the structure and meaning of the novel. In fact, this tale may stand both as emblem and synthesis for the entire work as it gathers together opposing meanings for the novel's central symbolic metaphor.

Little Dorrit invents the fairy tale as relief from the increasing internal and external pressure of Arthur's attentions and her growing love for him. She tells Maggy the story of a tiny woman, still "quite young," who keeps watch over a secret enclosed in a secret place in her tiny house. This secret is a shadow, "bright to look at." It is the shadow of someone who has gone away, and she cherishes it because "no one so good and kind had ever passed that way, and that was why in the beginning. She said, too, that nobody missed it, that nobody was the worse for it, that Some one had gone on to those who were expecting him . . . and that this remembrance was stolen or kept back from nobody" (p. 342). And it is a secret that dies with her.

Of course, we recognize that the tiny woman is Little Dorrit herself and that her love for Arthur is the bright, secret shadow that she hides in her prison room and in her secret heart. The tiny woman's house is a model for the story of Little Dorrit's and Arthur's love, nurtured within the heart, and later, within the walls of the Marshalsea, hidden until the hero finds eyes with which to see the love that has been present all along. Parallels between the lovers are embodied in the very language Little Dorrit uses to tell her self-effacing tale; she duplicates Arthur's language when he considers his secret, suppressed love for Pet Meagles ("nobody's heart was broken," etc.). And, later, Arthur will repeat her gesture as she moves away from the window at which she has been standing, "the sunset very bright upon her." She avoids the sun, for it reveals internal relevances for her fairy tale that she wishes to hide: "the sunlight flush was so bright on Little Dorrit's face when she came thus to the end of her story, that she interposed her hand to shade it" (p. 343). Thus the fairy tale anticipates the shift in meaning for the shadow that is to come, for here the shadow, now bright, stands for love.

Lyrical descriptions of the beauties and serenity of nature continue to gather force as the novel approaches its conclusion. A setting exceptional for its fullness of detail intensifies and dramatizes the shocking destruction of the Clennam house, seat of so many negative associations for the shadow motif:

> the clear steeples of the many churches looked as if they had advanced out of the murk that usually enshrouded them, and come much nearer. The smoke that rose into the sky had lost its dingy hue and taken a brightness upon it. The beauties of the sunset had not faded from

the long light films of cloud that lay at peace in the horizon. From a radiant centre, over the whole length and breadth of the tranquil firmament great shoots of light streamed among the early stars, like signs of the blessed later covenant of peace and hope that changed the crown of thorns into a glory. (p. 862)

The naturalized crown of thorns image helps prepare the way for the destruction of the source of negative connotations for the shadow motif of the novel; the catastrophe occurs in the long twilight of summer, as if nature herself is rising up spontaneously to cleanse the world of the blight represented by the Clennam house.

The closing scenes of the novel, which more and more resemble a series of static tableaux, represent a falling-off of artistic intensity in *Little Dorrit,* as the author manipulates his symbols to produce the required happy ending. The Marshalsea, now associated with maternal imagery, "embraces" Little Dorrit as she nurses Arthur back to emotional and spiritual health. This condition is first announced in the restoration of health to the natural world, now transformed from correlative for Arthur's dark symbolic journey into his past to sign of the healthy, golden autumn of the protagonists' lives: "On a healthy autumn day; when the golden fields had been reaped and ploughed again, when the summer fruits had ripened and waned, when the green perspectives of hops had been laid low by the busy pickers, when the apples clustering in the orchards were russet, and the berries of the mountain ash were crimson among the yellowing foliage" (p. 883). This passage, which opens the last chapter, presents the crescendo for the descriptions of nature in *Little Dorrit* in its fullness, richness, color. Though winter is coming, the scene is unrelievedly cheerful, with a wide vista opening out "clear and free." The ocean, too, returns, revitalized from its stagnation in the filthy harbor of Marseilles; "its thousand sparkling eyes were open, and its whole breadth was in joyful animation" (p. 883). Vision, once painful and to be avoided, is now also the source of joy. Clennam hears this message in Little Dorrit's voice which he now recognizes as the voice of his true mother, Nature. In the dramatic gesture that recalls Little Dorrit's reaction to her self-revelation in the fairy tale, "he put his hand over his eyes, murmuring that the light was strong upon them," and Little Dorrit rises to shade the window, moving close to his side in the softened light.

This scene prepares us for the novel's finale, when Little Dorrit comes "into the prison with the sunshine" (p. 893) on their wedding day. The joy of the closing is muted, appropriate to these wounded figures whose pasts have robbed them of so much possibility. They are married with the sun shining indirectly on them through the stained glass figure of Christ, attended by the representatives of the positive human community—Doyce, Pancks, Flora, Maggy, Meagles, and the Chiverys—who have helped restore Arthur to health. The symbols of sunlight and shadow, at last fully developed, fuse in the final sentences of the novel as Arthur and Little Dorrit descend into the arena of life, and "into a modest life of usefulness and happiness . . . in sunshine and shade. . . ."

The world has not altered, and yet, the ending seems to say, individual happiness is possible through the healing power of love. This message is partly supported by the primary symbolic motif of *Little Dorrit;* but, as I have argued, sunlight and shade are also used in subtle ways to undercut the happy outcome. The gradual metamorphosis of the darkness imagery in the novel into twilight and, still later, into fusion with the love elements indicates a diminished and rather sad view of the nature of love and joy in the world. The light of the book's finale, then, is not the bright light of passion, but, rather, the steady, moral light of self-knowledge and knowledge of the real world that comes of an acceptance of both light and darkness symbolizing the mixed nature of human life. The sunlight/shadow motif demonstrates this implied world view in *Little Dorrit* by its stylistic, thematic, and structural primacy.

This study of Dickens demonstrates his central importance to the development of word-painting in the nineteenth century. Dickens greatly expands its repertory of subjects and effects, and its increasingly fused relationship with its surrounding narrative. In general, visually composed description in Dickens develops in the direction of absorbing narrative and dramatic intent. But we must not make the mistake of assuming that this progress is uninterrupted. Even in his very last works, picturesque and symbolic word-paintings sometimes juxtapose. However, a chronological study of Dickens's novels clearly demonstrates a growing coherence among his narrative, dramatic, and descriptive modes as compared with the more traditional uses of word-paintings in the works of writers like Radcliffe and Scott.

Part Two

Word-Painting and Narrative in Poetry

3

Preview: Word-Painting in Thomson and Wordsworth

Just as Radcliffe's word-painting helps establish a fashion for extended visually oriented description in the novel, a brief comparison between representative word-paintings by Thomson and Wordsworth suggests the direction our feature takes in the poetic tradition. Radcliffe quotes extensively from Thomson in *The Mysteries of Udolpho: A Romance/Interspersed with Some Pieces of Poetry.* Both subtitle and borrowings suggest how heavily poets (including Thomson) influence novelists, though the genres are separated in my study for ease of discussion. Radcliffe borrows eight passages from Thomson to strengthen lyrical effects as epigraphs to chapters, and three more to intersperse with her narrative. Indicating authorial interest in formal generic issues akin to those tackled over two centuries later by Virginia Woolf in *The Waves, The Mysteries of Udolpho* represents the high point of Radcliffe's reliance on Thomson—along with Shakespeare, Milton and minor contemporary poets—to set the mood and to underscore picturesque word-painting.

The Seasons, Thomson's most important work, offers a gathering of eighteenth-century motifs and strategies upon which both novelists and poets could draw. Like Radcliffe, these poets typically employ an organizing rationale that alternates modes; but, characteristically for poetry, description, rather than narration, alternates with reflection. The "picture gallery" analogy aptly characterizes a poetic form descending from Chaucer and Spenser, passing through Thomson via Tennyson's segmented structures to the Symbolists and T. S. Eliot.

Thomson and Wordsworth help provide a proper context for Tennyson's subsequent innovations in word-painting and its integration into the evolving structures of narrative poetry. Since Thomson rarely includes extended ongoing narrative structures in his long poems, this discussion of his poetry will focus only on his contributions to the formal development of word-painting itself. Wordsworth's, in contrast, demonstrates a growing organic relevance of word-painting to long poems more narrative in nature.

The critic H. M. McLuhan theorizes that Thomson initiates, in the early eighteenth century, a new kind of Spenserian landscape poetry that searches for "significant art-emotion amidst natural scenes."[1] This impulse results in an evolution from a picturesque art of sensation to a kind of "paysage intérieur" in T. S. Eliot's poems and a new twentieth-century metaphysical poetry. Tennyson's work, which I will examine shortly in detail, occupies the midpoint in this line of development.

Although McLuhan slightly over-simplifies the history of this development, his comments correctly point to major shifts (over two centuries) in poetic depiction of landscape toward fusing scientific observation and psychological experience to achieve moments of intensely heightened perception. Thomson's contributions to the development of an iconic tradition in English poetry has been adequately characterized by Hagstrum, Cohen, Nicholson, Spencer, and others, who credit Thomson with introducing seventeenth-century landscape themes from the sublime canvases of Rosa and Claude into English poetry, much as Radcliffe utilized these images in the English novel.[2] According to Hagstrum, Thomson contributes to a tradition of landscape depiction in three major ways. First, he is able vividly to verbalize subtle effects of natural light, large-scale color, and natural motion. Secondly, he manages to describe a natural world that is simultaneously precisely particularized and idealized in a heroic manner. And, lastly, his nature descriptions are notable for the way in which he labors to solve the problem of landscape form.

Here, as an innovator of formal means, Thomson becomes important to this history of word-painting. His descriptions also offer us a baseline with which to compare later efforts to fuse description and narration in poetry, much as Radcliffe's did for fiction. As might be expected, Thomson's individual landscape "pictures," written in the same century as Radcliffe's, integrate with surrounding material in a method of organization that alternates modes, though Thomson alternates word-paintings with reflective passages and Radcliffe with predominantly narrative ones. This structure predates Tennyson's use of this segmented form throughout his career; "The Palace of Art" provides an instructive example of his work.

Since *The Seasons* presents one landscape picture after another, all of which reiterate similar motifs and present similar formal characteristics, one may pick passages nearly at random and still have a fair representation of his characteristic landscape themes and technique. Examine, for example, this passage from "Spring":

> But who can hold the shade, while Heaven descends
> In universal bounty, shedding herbs,
> And fruits, and flowers, on Nature's ample lap?
> Swift fancy fired anticipates their growth;
> And, while the milky nutriment distils,
> Beholds the kindling country colour round.[3]

(ll. 180–85)

An example of personification, this passage conceptualizes all the natural elements—heaven, nature, clouds, earth, and rain—in human terms at once both particular and idealized. The passage continues, describing sunset's sights and sounds, a rainbow, and a frolicsome boy.

> Till, in the western sky, the downward sun
> Looks out, effulgent, from amid the flush
> Of broken clouds, gay-shifting to his beam.
> The rapid radiance instantaneous strikes
> The illumined mountain; through the forest streams,
> Shakes on the floods, and in the yellow mist,
> Far smoking o'er the interminable plain,
> In twinkling myriads lights the dewy gems.
> Moist, bright, and green, the landscape laughs around.
> Full swell the woods; their every music wakes,
> Mix'd in wild concert with the warbling brooks
> Increased, the distant bleatings of the hills,
> And hollow lows responsive from the vales,
> Whence blending all the sweeten'd zephyr springs.
> Meantime, refracted from yon eastern cloud,
> Bestriding earth, the grand ethereal bow
> Shoots up immense; and every hue unfolds,
> In fair proportion, running from the red
> To where the violet fades into the sky.
> Here, awful Newton, the dissolving clouds
> Form, fronting on the sun, thy showery prism;
> And to the sage-instructed eye unfold
> The various twine of light, by thee disclosed
> From the white mingling maze. Not so the boy:
> He wondering views the bright enchantment bend,
> Delightful, o'er the radiant fields, and runs
> To catch the falling glory; but amazed
> Beholds the amusive arch before him fly,
> Then vanish quite away. Still night succeeds.

("Spring," ll. 189–218)

This passage demonstrates Thomson's famous skill at precisely capturing nuances of light and color in language. If, for example, one compares his description of rainbow-colored sunset with the gloomy sunset over the castle of Udolpho in Radcliffe's work at the climactic moment in the novel, one notes the greater visual precision of Thomson's descriptions. This passage also prefigures the Victorians' interest in incorporating scientific concepts into natural descriptions. Thomson combines references to Newton's *Opticks* (1704) and the new discoveries of the properties of light with a conventional sunset description.

The passage is alive with the poet's delight in very specific effects of light on the landscape. Yet Thomson's descriptions remain static catalogues rather than fully realized word-paintings. No clear ordering of the elements in this landscape provides the reader with a visual rationale. The description enumerates clouds, earth, sun, mountain, plain, woods, brooks, sounds, breeze, rainbow, day, and night, often painted with flashes of brilliant detail. But the description lacks the animation of a quasi-cinematic technique that might have involved the organization of details by the drama of the moving eye. Clearly, that was not Thomson's interest. The final feature of the passage—the vignette of the charming child who tries to catch the rainbow—provides a flickering narrative possibility, but it is not developed in the poem. The emphasis in this passage remains on the natural world; the boy is incidental. This passage is typical of Thomson's lack of concern with narrative. A reading of *The Seasons* as a whole convinces the twentieth-century reader, schooled in narratives, of the unremitting monotony of a long poem comprised largely of such description and reflection unsupported by narrative.

Another example of Thomson's skill at capturing the look of landscape that encourages "art emotion" comes from a later passage that succeeds in organizing the description much more coherently than the previous examples, and indicates how vividly Thomson verbalizes subtle light, color, and kinetic effects in verse:

> Thus up the mount, in airy vision wrapt,
> I stray, regardless whither; til the sound
> Of a near fall of water every sense
> Wakes from the charm of thought; swift-shrinking back,
> I check my steps, and view the broken scene.
>   Smooth to the shelving brink a copious flood
> Rolls fair, and placid; where collected all,
> In one impetuous torrent, down the steep
> It thundering shoots, and shakes the country round.
> At first an azure sheet, it rushes broad;
> Then whitening by degrees, as prone it falls
> And from the loud resounding rocks below
> Dash'd in a cloud of foam, it sends aloft
> A hoary mist, and forms a ceaseless shower.
> Nor can the tortured wave here find repose
> But, raging still amid the shaggy rocks,
> Now flashes o'er the scatter'd fragments, now
> Aslant the hollowed channel rapid darts;
> And falling fast from gradual slope to slope,
> With wild infracted course, and lessen'd roar,
> It gains a safer bed, and steals, at last,
> Along the mazes of the quiet vale.

("Summer," ll. 585–605)

Thomson manages to describe a world simultaneously particularized and idealized heroically. His organizational mode borrows from Baroque and Renaissance landscape the tendency to humanize and mythologize nature.

This passage is justly famous for its skillful verbalization of the effects of natural motion. Predating Burke's important statement on the sublime and the beautiful in 1757, Thomson depicts vastness in landscape through dramatizing the eye's movements as it follows the downward progression of a waterfall from the mountain top where the poet stands, to the peaceful valley below. The poet carefully moves us from the dreamlike, or visionary, mood of the wanderer to the kinetic energy of the waterfall, and then back to the peacefully running water at the base, which twists through the mazes of the vale in the irregular, serpentine lines so admired by the period.

Although Thomson describes what he sees clearly and objectively, there is very little sense of the inner nature of this observer. A more intimate participation in the natural setting as correlative for an observer's mental state awaits early Romantic poets such as Wordsworth. Such a shift in interest also dictates a formal change from single to multiple viewpoints of a given scene which characterizes the expressive aesthetic of nineteenth- and twentieth-century art. Word-painting, of course, reflects a poet's attitude toward nature; and a comparison between Thomson and Wordsworth affirms the growing fragmentation both of the relationship between man and nature and the expression of this shattering relationship in new segmented poetic forms. At the same time, the comparison highlights Wordsworth's and Coleridge's increasing interest in narrative verse as rigid formal poetics progressively loosen.

A chronological study of Wordsworth's poetic development indicates his rather abrupt declaration of independence from the eighteenth-century picturesque aesthetic by 1792, when he changed the name of an early collection from *Picturesque* to *Descriptive Sketches*. Indeed, the poet repudiates the picturesque strategy in a famous note: "Whoever, in attempting to describe their sublime features (The Alps), should confine himself to the cold rules of painting would give his reader but a very imperfect idea of those emotions which they have the irrisistible [*sic*] power of communicating to the most passive imaginations" (I, 85n.62).[4]

What form and content in Wordsworth's poems demonstrate his new strategy for word-painting? Two famous word-paintings from Wordsworth must suffice to demonstrate the shift from eighteenth-century to Romantic iconography in word-painting and the motif's relationship with narrative verse. In "Tintern Abbey"—a narrative of the progress in the growth of the poet's imagination to be amplified later in *The Prelude*—the word-painting that opens the poem represents an optimistic reading of the "thereness" of an external landscape (a continuing philosophical problem for this poet) that will exactly balance the cooperative workings of the creative imagination as it pictures the scene. Later, in the passage below from *The Prelude,* the relationship between word-painting and narrative becomes vastly more complicated when the visually described concrete scene is itself transcended by an apocalyptic moment that by its very nature obliterates the senses themselves.

"Tintern Abbey" begins with a description of what the poet sees as he sits beneath a sycamore on the banks of the Wye in spring, 1798, after a five-year absence. At first glance, the deceptively simple scene resembles a standardized, domesticated eighteenth-century poetic landscape.

> The day is come when I again repose
> Here, under this dark sycamore, and view
> These plots of cottage-ground, these orchard-tufts,
> Which at this season, with their unripe fruits,
> Are clad in one green hue, and lose themselves
> 'Mid groves and copses. Once again I see
> These hedge-rows, hardly hedge-rows, little lines
> Of sportive wood run wild: these pastoral farms,
> Green to the very door; and wreaths of smoke
> Sent up, in silence, from among the trees!
> With some uncertain notice, as might seem
> Of vagrant dwellers in the houseless woods,
> Or of some Hermit's cave, where by his fire
> The Hermit sits alone.

(ll. 9–22)

But new elements in Wordsworth's word-painting include the emphasis on a precisely placed "I" in the landscape. The dark vertical sycamore frames a landscape structured by the viewer's perspective, and the insistence on "again" (lines 1 and 6) draws attention to the drama of return. The poet, a figure in this landscape, scans the cultivated scene in an organized fashion, moving from foreground to follow a number of horizontal sightlines into the distance, from the river to the "hedge-rows, hardly hedge-rows, little lines / Of sportive wood run wild." This line implies two different views of the same scene, one a mental construct held fondly over time, the other, its present features. Carlos Baker calls this an effect of "double exposure,"[5] which expands our cinematic metaphor; and L. J. Swingle characterizes this passage as representing "the drama of indecision."[6]

This reading of our passage underscores the way in which Wordsworth's word-painting states in small the message of "Tintern Abbey": that the poet discovers what to make of nature in a process fusing perception and imagination. In a subtle way, the organization of this particular landscape description provides a visual analogue for the poet's striving for understanding. As he activates horizontal elements in the landscape—the plots, hedge-rows, and the River Wye itself—the eye embarks on a metaphorical journey that will provide the underlying organization for the meditative poem to follow. The poet will gradually see what nature can teach him. Thus the visual journey is simultaneously literal and symbolic, with vertical accents suggesting the possibility of a spiritual identity between poet, nature, and God.

The word-painting that begins "Tintern Abbey" thus provides entry into the meaning of the poem itself; its contribution is essential and cannot be extracted from the overall shape of the poem without a loss in vigor and concreteness. Wordsworth makes his verbal visualization an integral part of the narrative of self-discovery and the thematic meaning of the poem. With it, one embarks upon a study of nineteenth-century writers who relate narration to description more organically than had been the case in word-painters of the previous century.

The Prelude represents Wordsworth's most successful attempt to work out the ramifications of his central theme in a long poem. The subtitle of *The Prelude* announces the essentially narrative structure of the work: "Growth of a Poet's Mind (An Autobiographical Poem)." Throughout the poem, Wordsworth "journeys" toward an understanding of how creation depends upon the cooperative workings of mind and the external world, or of the imagination and nature. But this essentially narrative structure moves by fits and starts; most of the poem takes a distinctly meditative cast, as the poet philosophizes about possible meanings for seminal experiences in his life.

Among these seminal experiences are moments Wordsworth calls "spots of time," visionary moments usually achieved when the imagination has been aroused by fear or awe inspired by wild natural scenes, often in mist, darkness, or storm, manifestations of the sublime. One might expect to find word-paintings at such moments of heightened visual awareness and ecstasy, when the poet achieves sustained communion with nature. But, although the reader of Wordsworth remembers vividly these "spots of time," the student of word-painting quickly discovers that these spots are not so much visual as they are psychological phenomena. And, indeed, being visionary, they presuppose a blotting-out of the immediate sense impressions for a more cosmic one.

Such moments in *The Prelude* focus more on the poet's sense of awe and his "lesson" than they do on a moment of "frozen time" precisely and sensuously described. The vividness of impression derives, not from the extended visually oriented description that we have defined as a word-painting, but, rather, from the accumulation of a number of brief images of isolated phenomena such as the gibbet mast, or the girl with the pitcher in the moorland waste in Book XII. Items are pinpointed in this landscape, but they exist in the spotlighted isolation of a dream, unrelated to the surrounding landscape. They often capture the sense of heightened intensity of vision at moments of emotional crisis. For example, later in Book XII when Wordsworth recalls his reaction to the news of his father's death, he, significantly, pictures:

> The single sheep, and the one blasted tree,
> And the bleak music from that old stone wall,
> The noise of wood and water, and the mist
> That on the line of each of those two roads
> Advanced in such indisputable shapes;
> All these were kindred spectacles and sounds
> To which I oft repaired, and thence would drink,
> As at a fountain; . . .[7]

(ll. 319–26)

This image, while vivid, presents fragments of reality from which the poet can reconstruct the emotion he felt, and its lesson for growth. It is not developed pictorially on a scale extensive enough to qualify as a word-painting, but it does allude to the senses of sound, touch, and taste to amplify the primarily visual impression.

Swingle makes much of the "pictorial impulse" in Wordsworth but retains my emphasis (that is, that the "pictures" this poet creates are less immediately interesting visually than they are a "picture of the mind"). In this activity Wordsworth ascribes to the act of picturing an awesome power akin to that of God's creativity in order to prove that "the mind . . . is not of this world."[8] Such a claim puts considerable pressure on the poet to find emblems of creation in the external world. For the most part, Wordsworth's descriptions of nature exemplify the fitful achievement of such ecstatic moments, and serve to illustrate the way in which the poet understands the nature of his adult vision: "I see by glimpses now; when age comes on, / May scarcely see at all" (*Prelude,* XII, 281–82). Against this frightening possibility of the loss of the poet's visionary powers, he puts the power of these past moments of inspiration to prove restorative in the future.

While most of the spots of time do not adhere to our definition of word-painting, therefore, two interesting extended visually oriented passages both interpret characteristic motifs of mountain scenery and provide climactic moments of vision for the poet. These passages—one describing the gloomy strait upon which the poet stumbles after being lost in the Simplon Pass while crossing the Alps (Book VI), the other recording the poet's climactic Pisgah vision atop Mount Snowdon (Book XIV)—are outstanding for visually oriented details that create successful word-paintings in the sequential and orderly method of their visualization. These two passages are simultaneously two climactic moments in the narrative of the growth of the poet. Geoffrey H. Hartman calls them "two rival high-points of *The Prelude,*"[9] expressing not only the central meanings of this work, but also the poet's mature understanding of the workings of nature and the imagination, a problem that had haunted him throughout his creative life. Thus, in locating two of Wordsworth's most important word-paintings, one also rather neatly finds a locus for meaning in the overall narrative of self. And so, an analysis of the most visually oriented one of these passages reveals both new developments of our feature and the increasingly close relationship between word-paintings and narrative at the opening of the nineteenth century.

We have already spoken of the way in which mountain scenery provides an emblem of the Burkean sublime in the second half of the eighteenth century. In both Books VI and XIV of *The Prelude,* visionary moments associated with sublime landscapes—accompanied by awe or fear—precede or concretize a new stage in the development of the poet's understanding. In the first of these, the poet describes his journey across the Alps. He views Mont Blanc and the

Vale of Chamouny in a manner reminiscent of earlier picturesque poets. But the sublime now presents a mind-numbing "soulless image." An also static Vale "with its dumb cataracts and streams of ice, a motionless array of mighty waves" juxtaposes with the motions of "five rivers broad and vast," which

> made rich amends
> And reconciled us to realities;
> There small birds warble from the leafy trees,
> The eagle soars high in the element,
> There doth the reaper bind the yellow sheaf,
> The maiden spread the haycock in the sun,
> While Winter like a well-tamed lion walks,
> Descending from the mountain to make sport
> Among the cottages by beds of flowers.

(VI, ll. 532–40)

Vignettes of man's ordinary life orient the poet and guard him from the terrors of the inchoate sublime. These vignettes remind one of the personifying imagination of Thomson, and recall an earlier poetry.

How different, though, is the synthesizing imagination of the fully engaged poetic vision when Wordsworth describes his moment of vision as he stumbles upon the "gloomy strait" after becoming lost in the Simplon Pass while crossing the Alps. Here, the sublime presents for Wordsworth a mind-numbing "soulless image." The word-painting, charged with the overflow of powerful feelings occasioned by the experience itself, represents a reward in visual acuity for the leap in insight that follows. Its iconographic coherence help convince the reader of its aptness as an emblem of Eternity.

The poet journeys slowly through the gloomy strait, an enclosure that contrasts dramatically with the expansive image of infinitude. This landscape soon takes on the quality of a timeless world framed by ordinary experience.

> Downwards we hurried fast,
> And, with the half-shaped road which we had missed,
> Entered a narrow chasm. The brook and road
> Were fellow-travellers in this gloomy strait,
> And with them did we journey several hours
> At a slow pace. The immeasurable height
> Of woods decaying, never to be decayed,
> The stationary blasts of waterfalls,
> And in the narrow rent at every turn
> Winds thwarting winds, bewildered and forlorn,
> The torrents shooting from the clear blue sky,
> The rocks that muttered close upon our ears,
> Black drizzling crags that spake by the way-side
> As if a voice were in them, the sick sight
> And giddy prospect of the raving stream,
> The unfettered clouds and region of the Heavens,

> Tumult and peace, the darkness and the light—
> Were all like workings of one mind, the features
> Of the same face, blossoms upon one tree;
> Characters of the great Apocalypse,
> The types and symbols of Eternity,
> Of first, and last, and midst, and without end.
>
> (VI, ll. 619–40)

The winding path organizes visual progression through a clearly defined space whose organizing rationale operates by the opposition of elements: heights and depths, "stationary blasts of waterfalls," woods simultaneously decaying and eternal, motion and stasis. These elements exist in a nearly unbearable tension clearly generated by the internal state of the perceiver. But here, at last, the poet can grasp intuitively the fusion of all elements in this charged landscape, and the very oppositions themselves finally yield a visionary moment of Eternity which reconciles all opposites. The closure of the final image in our excerpt merges an abstract concept and its concrete visualization through the word-painting, to which all senses contribute fully.

This complicated passage represents a formal advancement in the relationship between descriptive and narrative materials. Details from the natural world, fused as a kind of reward for insight, are described clearly and coherently for their own sakes. Simultaneously, they assume climactic significance for the narrative of the poet's imaginative growth.

In contrast with Thomson's word-painting strategies in *The Seasons,* Wordsworth depends for structural coherence on the quality of vision in the speaker and on his subjective responses to a domestic or a wild natural scene. The viewer's eye systematically scanning a landscape establishes an anchor in reality for the more abstract meditations that comprise the majority of Wordsworth's major poems. He transforms visual detail by fusing outward forms and internal significance to capture essentially nonvisual insights. The details of a Wordsworthian landscape are vivid and interesting not only in themselves, but because the poet suggests their significance.

Wordsworth's word-paintings participate actively in the narrative impulse of his long poems. Organized as a journey through time and space, each verbal visualization echoes in miniature the overall progress of the work. Though overpowered by the meditative and narrative sections, these word-paintings focus moments of heightened states of consciousness. They carry a weight different from the eighteenth-century word-paintings of Thomson, Radcliffe, and Scott. Wordsworth's development of the feature suggests the direction Victorian word-painting was to take, and the immediate inheritance of Tennyson.

4

Tennyson

(Nor these alone,) but every landscape fair,
As fit for every mood of mind,
Or gay, or grave, or sweet, or stern, was there
Not less than truth designed.

"The Palace of Art"

Introduction

A chronological study of early, middle and late word-paintings in Dickens's novels indicates his growing fusion of descriptive and narrative modes as he moves toward a more symbolic art. The general development of Tennyson, the other Victorian writer emphasized in the present study, compares interestingly with the development of Dickens's word-paintings. Tennyson's word-paintings show a startling constancy in content, especially regarding their visual motifs. Unlike those of Dickens, Tennyson's word-paintings remain fairly consistent in terms of content; but, like Dickens, Tennyson increasingly integrates descriptive and narrative materials. His mature poetry exhibits a mastery of acute perception, economically phrased, that grants more attention to the appropriate coherence among modes.

Throughout a long and varied poetic career, Tennyson searched constantly for new poetic forms that might bridge the genres of poetry, fiction, and drama. Often he included social commentary as well. Fairly early, Tennyson became restless with poetic modes he clearly found restricting, such as ballads and sonnets, though he tried his hand at nearly every traditional poetic form. His fascination with narratives provides the impetus for his search for new poetic forms from "Armageddon" to *Idylls of the King*. This search for a poetic form that might embrace lyrical, dramatic, and narrative modes constitutes Tennyson's main contribution to the blending of genres that characterizes many late nineteenth- and early twentieth-century literary works. In addressing the nagging problem of how to breach the limitations of genre, he is strikingly close to concerns of Modernist writers like Virginia Woolf and T. S. Eliot, to whose works I will briefly refer later by way of conclusion. The tension that is inherent in their attempt to fuse lively storytelling with a primarily lyrical genius haunts all three of these writers; and it produces structural weaknesses apparent in some of their major works.

Even the titles of Tennyson's longer poetical works, beginning publication in 1847, indicate his struggle to express new "hybrid" poetic forms: *The Princess: A Medley; Maud: A Monodrama; In Memoriam: Fragments of an Elegy;* and *Idylls of the King.* A chronological survey of his collected poetry suggests that panel structures and fragmented forms begin to express his poetic vision more accurately than did the shorter lyrics of his early poetry. Tennyson is central to a study of Victorian word-painting for two primary reasons. First, throughout his career, one of his greatest poetic strengths is his ability to conjure up vivid and varied word-paintings; he may well be the greatest word-painter of them all! Secondly, his solutions to problems of fusing lyric, narrative, and dramatic verse suggest fruitful directions to poetic experimenters who came after him. Tennyson's most successful landscapes rely on the clear visual perspective of a particular viewer. His ability simultaneously to evoke a vivid mental picture and to suggest the mental or psychological state of the viewer constitutes an innovative means of relating lyric, descriptive, and narrative materials.

Tennyson's word-paintings demonstrate remarkably consistent iconography throughout his long and extremely productive poetic career. My study first establishes the characteristics of this poet's extended visually oriented descriptions by choosing judiciously from his collected works. The discussion will move chronologically—so far as it is possible to do so—from juvenilia through the early poems of 1830, 1832, and 1842 to the *English Idylls,* and then to the longer poems of Tennyson's mature years: *The Princess, In Memoriam,* and *Idylls of the King.* At each point, not only will I suggest the characteristic subjects and formal properties of individual word-paintings, but I will discuss their relationship to the surrounding narrative and ways in which this relationship explores innovative poetic forms.

With the exception of *Idylls of the King,* which represents a recapitulation of nearly all Tennyson's characteristic word-painting, a study of the development of this feature in Tennyson's poetry reveals an uncanny similarity to the development of the feature in the representative novels of Dickens that we examined earlier. As do Dickens's early novels, Tennyson's early poetry relies heavily on the picturesque and sublime conventions for landscape tradition so popular in late eighteenth-century poetry. It is to be expected that writers would mimic established subjects and modes in their apprenticeships. But the gradual shift from early picturesque description to what the critic McLuhan calls "paysage intérieur"[1] strikingly resembles the development we have noticed in the works of Dickens. Not only that, but techniques for visualizing moments of

dramatic climax in Tennyson's *English Idylls* and *Idylls of the King* are strikingly close to Dickens's use of verbal tableau in the works of his middle and
late periods.

Early Poems: An Iconography of Landscape

Tennyson's first extended visually oriented description introduces the iconography of the sea—in storm or calm aftermath—which he was to scene-paint
often throughout his career. It appears in *The Devil and the Lady,* a verse-
drama chiefly memorable for the fact that Tennyson wrote it when he was four-
teen years old.

> The black storm—
> From out whose mass of volumed vapour sprang
> The lively curling thunderbolt—had ceased
> Long ere from out the dewy depth of Pines
> Emerging on the hollowed banks, that bound
> The leapings of the saucy tide, I stood—
> The mighty waste of moaning waters lay
> So goldenly in moonlight, whose clear lamp
> With its long line of vibratory lustre
> Trembled on their dun surface, that my Spirit
> Was buoyant with rejoicings. Each hoar wave
> With crispèd undulation arching rose,
> Thence falling in white ridge with sinuous slope
> Dashed headlong to the shore and spread along
> The sands its tender fringe of creamy spray.[2]
>
> (ll. 72–86)

Although this passage echoes with references to *The Tempest* and *Comus,*[3]
many essential features of Tennyson's word-paintings are also already present.
Violent storms at sea often set the scene in Tennyson's poems for the appearance of the speaker through whose perspective we view it, a *modus operandi*
borrowed from the pastoral conventions of classical poetry. Tennyson often
opens early narrative or dramatic poems with a word-painting (see, for example, "Mariana," "The Lady of Shalott," or "Oenone"), creating space for the
speaker. In addition to relying upon its classical overtones, the passage from
The Devil and the Lady relies heavily on the conventions of the eighteenth-century sublime in its description of the storm with its dramatic contrast between
blackness, accompanied by the sound of thunderbolts, and golden moonlight
soaking the storm's peaceful aftermath.

   The Devil and the Lady introduces several other characteristics of Tennyson's word-paintings. First, Tennyson often poses the viewer where land and
water meet. In *The Devil and the Lady,* for example, the magus, dwarfed by
the immensity of the ocean (another motif derived from the sublime), stands on

the banks of the "hoary tide," watching the waves dash on the shore. Later in his writing, Tennyson will tighten the dramatic contrast between enclosure and expansion, between heights and depths, by typically placing his observer on a high prospect, looking, deep in thought, on the vastness below (see "Oenone," for example). Here, in Tennyson's earliest word-painting, the speaker emerges from "the dewy depth of Pines," a movement that offers dramatic contrast between dark, enclosed background space and the endless vista ahead.

The fusion of the auditory and the visual—sometimes augmented by the tactile and other senses as well—represents another important feature of Tennyson's word-painting. The magus hears the thunderbolt, notes "the mighty waste of moaning waters," and watches the waves dashing on the shore, a series of vivid visual and aural impressions that build an effective description of the scene. Like Radcliffe, Wordsworth, and Dickens, Tennyson often supports his word-paintings with an appropriate auditory accompaniment. In addition, the rhythm of later word-paintings adds significantly to the sensuous effect of such "pictures," although this rhythmic element is notably missing in most of Tennyson's juvenilia.

The framing of the word-painting constitutes the last characteristic feature of Tennyson's method that the passage from *The Devil and the Lady* suggests. Here, pine-woody darkness provides the background—and the horizon, the boundaries—of vision. Both frame and the motionless, observing figure of the magus provide a still-point from which to observe the dramatic movement of the ocean after storm.

This scene often appears, with variations, in Tennyson's poetry. Its iconography and its compositional method are elements to which Tennyson, with his habit of "self-borrowing," often returns. Often a motionless viewer observes some of Tennyson's favorite visual motifs: the vast spaces of reflecting water or of mountain prospect, moonlight drenching a scene, the recurrent rhythms of waves breaking on sand. Tennyson also characteristically contrasts motion and stasis, darkness and light, height and depth, enclosure and expansion, and form (clarity of line) and formlessness (vastness and obscurity). The feature of visual distinctness and indistinctness will become especially important in late poems such as *In Memoriam* and *Idylls of the King,* where it will metaphorically connote intellectual, moral, or ethical insight or blindness.

But what of the relationship between word-painting and narrative in Tennyson's earliest word-painting? Here, we see one of the chief deficiencies of Tennyson's apprenticeship poetry, for the passage is poorly served by its poetic environment. The poetic lines immediately preceding and following the passage we have just examined miss the opportunity to emphasize the dramatic significance of the framed "moment." Undigested narrative detail comes before:

> *Magus:*   Half the powers o' the other world
> Were leagued against my journeying: but had not
> The irresistible and lawless might

> Of brazen-handed fixed Fatality
> Opposed me, I had done it.
>
> (ll. 68–72)

And a second storm, undifferentiated from the first, follows:

> Thereat my shallop lightly I unbound,
> Spread my white sail and rode exulting on
> The placid murmurings of each feathery wave
> That hurried into sparkles round the cleaving
> Of my dark Prow; but scarcely had I past
> The third white line of breakers when a squall
> Fell on me from the North, an inky Congress
> O' the Republican clouds unto the zenith
> Rushed from the horizon upwards with great speed
> Of their own thunderbolts.
>
> (ll. 87–96)

The loose structure of this verse drama detracts from the effectiveness of the word-painting, and action receives greater emphasis than do the effects of vision on the main character. The diction is inflated and artificial ("vibratory lustre," for example) and genuine thought or feeling is noticeably absent. The word-paintings of Tennyson's mature years are much more integrally related to their surrounding narrative than the awkward passage we have just examined. But this passage establishes some characteristic motifs and methods of Tennysonian word-painting.

Two additional examples from the juvenilia demonstrate Tennyson's early reliance on the conventional landscapes of the eighteenth-century sublime. Subsequent discussion will indicate the constancy of these descriptive themes throughout his poetic career. A wonderfully macabre Gothic poem, "The Vale of Bones," opens with an extended landscape description:

> Along yon vapour-mantled sky
> The dark-red moon is riding high;
> At times her beams in beauty break
> Upon the broad and silvery lake;
> At times more bright they clearly fall
> On some white castle's ruined wall;
> At times her partial splendour shines
> Upon the grove of deep-black pines,
> Through which the dreary night-breeze moans,
> Above this vale of scattered bones.
>
> (ll. 1–10)

Again the poet describes moon, lake and pines, accompanied by the auditory element ("dreary night-breeze moans"). However, here these motifs are added to a picturesque ruined castle and the grisly vale of bones. Written while Ten-

nyson was at Cambridge and printed only once (in 1827), the passage turns up
again, reworked into the song "The Splendour Falls on Castle Walls" in *The
Princess* (1847) with its Gothic excesses trimmed, and related somewhat more
organically to its segmented narrative.

In "On Sublimity" the poet requests, not "vales of tenderest green," but,
rather, "the wild cascade, the rugged scene, / The loud surge bursting o'er the
purple sea."[4] Again, the ingredients for a proper sublime landscape mix in such
passages as:

> I love your voice, ye echoing winds, that sweep
>> Through the wide womb of midnight, when the veil
> Of darkness rests upon the mighty deep,
>> The labouring vessel, and the shattered sail—
> Save when the forked bolts of lightening leap
>> On flashing pinions, and the mariner pale
> Raises his eyes to heaven.

(ll. 41–47)

But although many characteristic features appear, the description lacks both the
visual rationale for the order of details and the clear kinetic sense of a fully
realized word-painting.

In a demonstration of imaginative originality equal to the contrast between
Wordsworth's *Descriptive Sketches* and his *Lyrical Ballads of 1798,* Tennyson
burst upon the literary scene in 1830 with *Poems, Chiefly Lyrical.* This volume
includes outstanding poems such as "Mariana" and "The Kraken," along with
interesting, if flawed, lesser works such as "Supposed Confessions of a Second-Rate Sensitive Mind" and "Recollections of the Arabian Nights." Although
some of the poems in this collection continue to rely on the picturesque imagination we have noticed in Tennyson's juvenilia, "Mariana" and "The Kraken"
announce the deepening suggestiveness of Tennyson's poetic descriptions.
"Mariana" includes both simple visual images—the least complex kind of
poetic description—and visually oriented materials that serve simultaneously to
illuminate the object being described and the sensibility perceiving it. "The
Kraken," on the other hand, is a fine early example of Tennyson's interest in
visionary poetry. A fourth level of complexity for visually oriented description—visual images that appeal simultaneously to sensuous and intellectual understanding (such as Metaphysical poetry)—will appear much later in Tennyson's poetry, and I will note it in the discussion of *Idylls of the King.*

In contrast to the generalized landscapes of the sublime word-paintings
that dominate Tennyson's early poetic efforts, "Mariana" announces an approach to landscape description that is severely fragmented, deriving its effect
from the specificity of close examination of ordinary objects often considered
too insignificant to mention. Instead of expansive vista, "Mariana" opens with
an exceedingly contractive enumeration of eight disconnected objects in a landscape whose principle of organization is not at first clear.

> With blackest moss the flower-plots
>   Were thickly crusted, one and all:
> The rusted nails fell from the knots
>   That held the pear to the gable-wall.
> The broken sheds look'd sad and strange:
>   Unlifted was the clinking latch;
>   Weeded and worn the ancient thatch
> Upon the lonely moated grange.
>   She only said, 'My life is dreary,
>   He cometh not,' she said;
>   She said, 'I am aweary, aweary,
>   I would that I were dead!'

(ll. 1–12)

Flower-plots, nails, gable wall, shed, latch, thatch, and grange suggest a narrow focus and introduce the structural model for the poem: eight lines of sensuous description followed by a four-line balladic refrain that varied slightly to suggest Mariana's despair. The idiosyncratic visual perspective evokes curiosity in the reader concerning both the psychological state of this particular observer and the narrative explanation for her present state. Tennyson's use of word-painting to raise questions concerning psychological and narrative truths in a poem constitutes a maturing sophistication in this poet's technique.

Although Tennyson narrates the poem in the third person, Culler and others argue that the particular way in which the landscape is described convinces us that the entire poem is spoken by Mariana. Culler's explanation of the technique by which Tennyson achieves this perspective admirably summarizes recent critical thinking about the poem.

> It is her perception of the grange, the phenomenology of it, that we are given. Partly this is done through the images of brokenness and decay, of darkness and shadow, of emptiness and desolation, which are also the images of her mind. But partly, too, it is done through a prolonged sense of interior time. . . . The technical means by which this is done—chiefly the alternation of night and day, the use of verbs in the customary or habitual mode, the slight variations in the refrain which but emphasize its essential sameness, and the retardation of the meter—are deftly handled. But the chief resource in fusing subject and object is the utter absence in the poem of any guiding, organizing, or generalizing intelligence. The description consists entirely of isolated, atomistic detail.[5]

Culler's last point echoes the more narrowly focused study by Carol Christ (*The Finer Optic*), who studies the relationship between particularization and generalization in the poetry of Tennyson, Rossetti, Browning, and Hopkins. And both critics are indebted to the early work of Harold Bloom, who argued some years ago that the visual intensity of description in "Mariana" forces the reader to deduce heightened emotional states in the speaker to account for an "unnatural" vividness and intensity in the descriptive materials.[6] Bloom's work, which restates Ruskin's "pathetic fallacy," notes the displacement of unusual emotion from individual to landscape. Bloom also points to a similar use of sensuous images in *In Memoriam,* such as the description of the yew. He suggests Tennyson's skill at articulating static states of being such as ennui, lethargy, melancholy, and inertia.

Picturesque detail in "Mariana" takes on new significance when simple visual impressions suggest both phenomenological and psychological truths. Christ argues that in the case of "Mariana" and *Maud* (the only Tennyson poems she studies in detail), visually oriented specificity is meant to suggest the "morbid emotion" of the viewer.[7] The way in which objects are intensely visualized symbolizes "the loss of balance and proportion, the inability to integrate and order experience, and a consequent isolation in purely subjective perception" (p. 29). The fragmented word-painting that largely composes "Mariana," in other words, is far from a merely picturesque landscape—which Christ defines in general as "an emphasis on the pleasures of vision apart from any truth value they might contain" (p. 8)—but is, rather, a correlative for the incoherence of despair.

The "story" of Mariana is deliberately indeterminate. Nothing "happens" in the poem, but the refrain suggests that she wishes to die. Like many literary ballads—for example, Keats's *La Belle Dame sans merci*—this poem suggests a state of despair or death-in-life. But Tennyson sacrifices specificity of event to depiction of a generalized psychological state. Paradoxically, he succeeds in eliciting this generalized state by reference to extremely specific details in a desolate landscape. Word-painting in this poem simultaneously convinces the reader to accurately picture what Mariana sees and hears ("The blue fly sung in the pane," for example) and to feel her languor. The landscape accurately registers her stagnation and despair.

This poem represents Tennyson's first successful effort to use word-painting both to suggest a psychological state and to relate uniquely to the story that explains that state. Although "Mariana" cannot really be termed a "narrative," narrative fragments imply the woman's story, and word-painting here is more symbolic and visionary than picturesque. How delightful it would have been for the present writer, had "Mariana" been the product of Tennyson's middle or late years. Then, the poem might have been an example of Tennyson's developmental progression from picturesque to symbolic landscapes. But, so far, this close study of Tennyson's word-paintings indicates the consistency of motifs and his early appreciation of the usefulness of word-paintings to depict simultaneously the object perceived and the quality of the perceiver. As Tennyson masters technique, he will become increasingly successful at word-paintings and narrative in later poems.

Another of Tennyson's favorite subjects for word-paintings also appears in both his juvenilia and in *Poems, Chiefly Lyrical.* The visionary, the third kind of descriptive poetry previously mentioned, offers word-paintings that describe other-worldly visions whose outlines we have never seen. Yet the descriptions convince us of the possibilities for such visionary landscapes through a technique that fuses deliberate vagueness of some elements in the landscape with acute specificity of other details.

Tennyson paints many such visionary landscapes in the course of his career, from "Armageddon" and "Timbuctoo" through "The Kraken," to "The Holy Grail" and other visionary landscapes from *Idylls of the King*. Even some of his very last lyrics such as "The Ancient Sage" and "Merlin and the Gleam" incorporate allusions to other-worldly visions.

John D. Rosenberg asserts that "The Kraken" stakes out Tennyson's essential subject: "the twilight world of myth in which consciousness and unconsciousness intersect."[8] Tennyson's compositional method varies from poem to poem, but the critic Valerie Pitt notices that a peculiar combination of vivid foreground detail and background blurriness occurs in all. She attributes this feature to the poet's poor eyesight and conjectures that Tennyson really saw the world this way.[9] Yet in writing visionary poetry, Tennyson may simply combine traditional attitudes toward the visionary with his own keen interest in contemporary scientific discoveries concerning geological time and the enormity of Darwinian cycles of life. Certainly, Tennyson's visionary landscapes sometimes share the technique we have examined in the visionary passages from Wordsworth's *The Prelude,* where a dramatic use of misted and clarified vision illuminates both an external and internal landscape of thought and feeling. A similar treatment of visionary landscape is notable in *Idylls of the King*.

"Armageddon" represents an early version of a visionary landscape upon which Tennyson later drew for details in "The Coming of Arthur." The young poet vividly captures the hallucinatory acuteness of an other-worldly experience:

> . . . my mental eye grew large
> With such a vast circumference of thought,
> That, in my vanity, I seemed to stand
> Upon the outward verge and bound alone
> Of God's omniscience. Each failing sense,
> As with a momentary flash of light,
> Grew thrillingly distinct and keen. I saw
> The smallest Grain that dappled the dark Earth,
> The indistinctest atom in deep air,
> The Moon's white cities, and the opal width
> Of her small, glowing lakes, her silver heights
> Unvisited with dew of vagrant cloud,
> And the unsounded, undescended depth
> Of her black hollows.

(ll. 23–36)

Tennyson pays relatively more attention to the structure of the description here than he did in the earlier passage from *The Devil and the Lady* with which it shares certain iconographical motifs. This attention makes the passage from

"Armageddon" more visually acute than the earlier passage, even though it describes a private vision. In order to anchor the visionary moment in "Armageddon," Tennyson attempts to direct the viewer's mental eye to "circumference" and "verge," presenting the vision in terms that clearly contrast darkness and light, form and formlessness. The visual rationale in this passage is clear, for the description moves coherently from earth to air, to the moon with its "white cities," its lakes, mountains, and hollows. And, when Tennyson later reworks the passage from "Armageddon" for "Timbuctoo," he augments the beautiful distinctness with lines describing the galaxy and its supernatural lights in order to intensify even further the dramatic interplay of light and dark:

> The clear Galaxy
> Shorn of its hoary lustre, wonderful,
> Distinct and vivid with sharp points of light,
> Blaze within blaze, an unimagined depth
> And harmony of planet-girded Suns
> And moon-encircled planets, wheel in wheel,
> Arched the wan Sapphire.
>
> (ll. 103–9)

Paden notes that this passage "is apparently the first of Tennyson's references to that mystical experience which, occurring throughout his life, formed the personal basis of his faith."[10] Tennyson himself noted of such a moment that, "It is no nebulous ecstasy, but a state of transcendent wonder, associated with absolute clearness of mind" (Ricks, p. 176). On such a moment will the climax of *In Memoriam* later depend.

The examples cited thus far attest to Tennyson's continuing interest in visionary landscapes throughout his career. One of the most successful of these appears in the collection of 1830. "The Kraken" suggests apocalypse in a brief fifteen-line description of the fabled sea-monster who slumbers in the depths of the sea. James Welch points out that, here, landscape images two sorts of time: static and dynamic.[11] The poem's brevity and careful selection of significant detail help Tennyson avoid the structural excesses of the other early visionary poems I have just discussed.

> Below the thunders of the upper deep;
> Far, far beneath in the abysmal sea,
> His ancient, dreamless, uninvaded sleep
> The Kraken sleepeth: faintest sunlights flee
> About his shadowy sides: above him swell
> Huge sponges of millennial growth and height;
> And far away into the sickly light,
> From many a wondrous grot and secret cell
> Unnumbered and enormous polypi
> Winnow with giant arms the slumbering green.
> There hath he lain for ages and will lie

Battening upon huge seaworms in his sleep,
Until the latter fire shall heat the deep;
Then once by man and angels to be seen,
In roaring he shall rise and on the surface die.

Images of surface and depths, of sunlight and shadow, of oceanic movement combined with the absolute stasis of the sea-monster build a sense of dread in the reader, who may remember the moment predicted in Rev. 13:1, "And I stood upon the sand of the sea, and saw a beast rise up out of the sea."[12] The description of objects around the kraken (the sponges and polypi) attracts our attention away from a precise visualization of the sea creature, which adds to its sense of mystery. The combination of clarity and void helps account for the description's powerfully enigmatic effect. The kraken, mythological, becomes a symbol to link past prophecy with future catastrophe.

While post-Modernist critics concentrate on poems such as "Mariana" and "The Kraken," it is important to remember that *Poems, Chiefly Lyrical* contains mostly picturesque word-paintings. Indeed, it is fascinating to realize that Hallam, Tennyson's first and most important critic, fails even to mention these two poems in his first, appreciative review. Discussing Tennyson as a picturesque poet, and linking him with Keats and Shelley as "poets of sensation," Hallam concentrates, instead, on "Recollections of the Arabian Nights"! Important comments on Tennyson's use of the picturesque—an approach to landscape that concerns this study, since it represents the first stage in the history of word-painting—began with Arthur Henry Hallam's insightful early evaluation of Tennyson's art, "On Some of the Characteristics of Modern Poetry, and on the Lyrical Poems of Alfred Tennyson."[13] Here Hallam sketches "the five distinctive excellencies of Tennyson's manner."

First, his luxuriance of imagination, and at the same time his control over it. Secondly, his power of embodying himself in ideal characters, or rather moods of character, with such extreme accuracy of adjustment, that the circumstances of the narration seem to have a natural correspondence with the predominant feeling, and, as it were, to be evolved from it by assimilative force. Thirdly, his vivid, picturesque delineation of objects, and the peculiar skill with which he holds all of them fused, to borrow a metaphor from science, in a medium of strong emotion. Fourthly, the variety of his lyrical measures, and exquisite modulation of harmonious words and cadences to the swell and fall of the feelings expressed. Fifthly, the elevated habits of thought, implied in these compositions. (pp. 109–10)

The passage reminds one of the qualities Tennyson's contemporaries praised in his work. Hallam assumes that "Recollections of the Arabian Nights" will be the favorite poem from the collection of 1830, and, sounding the highest praise, calls the poem "a perfect gallery of pictures," because of the poet's "concise boldness, with which in a few words an object is clearly painted" (p. 96).

The two stanzas that Hallam singles out to demonstrate Tennyson's skill in painting "pictures," are the two outstanding visually oriented passages in this work which, in Hallam's words, captures the "mood" of childhood with the "solemn distinctness in every image." As the speaker glides down the Tigris in a dream vision on the "tide of time," he views with pleasure the panorama unfolding on the shore:

> Above through many a bowery turn
> A walk with vary-coloured shells
> Wandered engrained. On either side
> All round about the fragrant marge
> From fluted vase, and brazen urn
> In order, eastern flowers large,
> Some dropping low their crimson bells
> Half-closed, and others studded wide
>   With disks and tiars, fed the time
>   With odour in the golden prime
> Of good Haroun Alraschid.
>
> (ll. 56–66)

The structure provided by narrating a journey down the Tigris organizes a series of brightly colored scenes, with their exotic shapes and eastern fragrances, but the journey structure is distinctly secondary to the word-pictures themselves. In this poem, sight fuses with the sense of smell to produce a pleasing mixture of sensations. Later in the poem, when the speaker walks through the gardens of Haroun Alraschid, he gazes, transfixed ("with dazed vision") at a glorious fairy-tale architecture (stanza 12) in which flame-lit windows contrast with "hollow-vaulted dark" and the streaming glory of a crescent-decorated roof. The poem culminates in a vision of the Caliph and a strangely alluring Persian girl, after which, in silence, the poem breaks off, denying narrative. The poem's movement, in keeping with childlike dreams, is disconnected, focusing neither on coherent narrative nor on psychological complexity. Both structure and imagery suggest elements that will reappear in later Tennyson poems such as "The Palace of Art" and parts of *The Princess* and *In Memoriam*. But word-painting in "Recollections of the Arabian Nights" looks back to the picturesque tradition I have been sketching, rather than forward to a more integrally related symbolic technique.

One last example from *Poems, Chiefly Lyrical* indicates a future direction for visually oriented poetry in Tennyson. In the long, tormented monologue, "Supposed Confessions of a Second-Rate Sensitive Mind," formlessness—a traditional image of sublimity—becomes fearful as an image of self:

> What if
> Thou pleadest still, and seest me drive
> Through utter dark a full-sailed skiff,
> Unpiloted i' the echoing dance

Of reboant whirlwinds, stooping low
Unto the death, not sunk!
....
I think that pride hath now no place
Nor sojourn in me. I am void,
Dark, formless, utterly destroyed.

(ll. 93–98, 120–22)

Again one notes the iconography of sea and skiff, sounding like similar visual motifs from *The Devil and the Lady,* but, in a dramatic tightening of word-painting and narrative, the pilotless boat has become internalized as a motif of self-doubt.

Thus far, this study of Tennyson has established basic features of his early word-paintings and has asserted that the essential elements of his visually oriented descriptions are present fairly early. His juvenilia and *Poems, Chiefly Lyrical* contain at least three of the four basic kinds of descriptive poetry: simple visual images, images suggestive of a state of mind ("Mariana"), and visionary landscapes ("The Kraken"). Now that some of the basic features of Tennyson's word-paintings have been established here, subsequent discussion will focus on their relationship to narrative (which increasingly interested the poet in his mature years).

A brief examination of those major poems published first in 1832—but extensively revised for the collection published after Tennyson's "ten-year's silence," in 1842—indicates how the poet trimmed some of the excesses characteristic of his early word-paintings in order to integrate description with narration. Increasingly, Tennyson moves away from long set pieces of descriptive poetry and toward briefer, but more suggestive, description that contributes important material both to form and content of particular poems. "By 1842," Edgar F. Shannon notes, "Tennyson was in complete control of his poetic purpose and resources."[14] Poems important to the argument that his control shapes both description and narration in Tennyson's work include "The Lady of Shalott," "The Lotos-Eaters," "The Palace of Art," "Ulysses," "Morte d'Arthur" and *English Idylls.* The last of these will receive attention in the next section of this discussion, since it represents the addition of verbal tableaux to Tennyson's visually oriented descriptions.

"The Lady of Shalott" represents Tennyson's most concentrated recounting of a fairy-tale narrative in four brief sections. Again, he relies primarily on the visual sense, but augments this with the auditory. The figure overlooking a prospect from a high cliff has been replaced here by the immured maiden who views an exterior scene only obliquely. Like Mariana, she is isolated, but there is no brooding, internalized landscape in "The Lady of Shalott." Instead, the poem opens with a picturesque landscape scene which later readers of the poem called "Pre-Raphaelite," because of its preternatural brightness and clarity and its deliberately archaic syntax.

On either side the river lie
Long fields of barley and of rye,
That clothe the wold and meet the sky;
And through the field the road runs by
   To many-towered Camelot;
And up and down the people go,
Gazing where the lilies blow
Round an island there below,
   The island of Shalott.

(I, ll. 1–9)

In this ballad, perspective determines both scale and theme. The Lady, high in her tower, mirrors reality, turning it into a series of tapestry pictures. At the poem's climax, when (lured by her own loneliness and the sight of Sir Lancelot) she turns to look directly out the window, she loses the ordering of her perceptions and must die, cursed by some indeterminate fate. Shannon's interesting article tries to reconcile the many interpretations of this poem by following the ambiguity of images associated with the Lady (e.g. the suggestion that appearances deceive in the opening landscape, the self-indulgent aspects of the Lady's bower, and her life-denying service to art) and contrasting them with primarily positive religious and visual images associated with Lancelot. Noting that "light, Lancelot's primary attribute, is in Tennyson's poetry invariably the image for a spiritual state of perfection or for the manifestation of Divinity" (p. 213), Shannon concludes that, "The Lady's final vision resolves the ambiguity of appearance and reality posed by the opening landscape of the poem. Passing from sight to insight through three stages of perception in ascending order of truth—indirect, direct and mystical—she grasps behind the phenomena the reality of which Tennyson himself was certain" (p. 218). Thus, Shannon argues convincingly that the poem celebrates "commitment over detachment and expressive over mimetic art" (p. 208).

The opening word-painting at once announces Tennyson's mastery of suggestive detail and strongly patterned rhythmical structure. The first section of the poem gives an external perspective on the Lady's environs, narrated in the iterative present tense. Much like a medieval emblem book, a peaceful rural scene stretches before the reader, and details like "willows whiten," turning up their leaves in the breeze, convince us of the sharp focus of the verbal picture. Section II brings the reader within "four gray walls, and four gray towers" where one shares the Lady's perspective on the scene. The same landscape, introduced in Section I, appears only through a mirror that reflects "shadows of the world." Color from this outside world is bright and primary: red, yellow, blue. Although these visual pictures are clear, the Lady herself remains shadowy, for, like the technique in "The Kraken," we never look directly at her in her tower, but only at her accessories. Section II ends with her announcement that she is "half sick of shadows."

This psychological state prepares both Lady and reader for the appearance of Lancelot in Section III. He enters the poem, dazzling in flame and gold, like a star in the purple night.[15] His strong, cheerful song combines with her fairy song in the first part of the poem to dramatize the fusion of sound and sight in this deceptively simple ballad. Sight, however, is still primary, and causes the denouement: when the Lady looks directly at world of man and nature, "the curse is come upon" her.

Section IV begins with a brief word-painting to balance the cheerful summer landscape of the poem's opening. With the curse, the Lady enters the world of time and death, and the cycle of nature turns from summer to autumn:

> In the stormy east-wind straining,
> The pale yellow woods were waning,
> The broad stream in his banks complaining,
> Heavily the low sky raining
> Over towered Camelot

(IV, ll. 1–5)

Descending from her tower, she embarks by boat upon the river of time, singing her expressive death song. The poem's action concludes when Lancelot, not knowing who she is, nevertheless is touched by something in her lovely face, and muses upon her death.

The pared-down simplicity of stanzaic structure and the tight rhyme scheme (aaaabccb) enhances Tennyson's control over both description and the forward narration of the action in this poem. Clear, visually oriented descriptive materials balance perfectly with the requirements of vivid story telling in the balladic tradition, in which individual moments create a structure of discrete sections whose interconnections are left unstated. By moving the story from late summer to fall, the landscape suggests the approach of death and mirrors human actions in nature's sympathies. By threading a number of sharply realized visual pictures through the poem, Tennyson causes word-painting to contribute significantly to the evocation of an earlier, simpler oral poetry.

"Oenone" and "The Lotos-Eaters," like "The Lady of Shalott," rely on a dramatic story to keep the poem moving along; but in the case of these two contemporaneous poems, Tennyson increasingly leans upon the structure of myth. Both mythic poems successfully incorporate extended visual pictures into their narrations, but with opposite narrative effects. "Oenone" emphasizes the story of how Paris abandons Oenone for Helen of Troy (a narrative that progresses in a linear fashion), whereas all the images in "The Lotos-Eaters" reinforce a mood of inaction, stasis, and stagnation. Both poems, however, center upon a single decisive moment of choice. And in both poems, word-painting mirrors theme.

"Oenone" represents both Tennyson's reworking of what Rick calls "the pastoral love-lament—hopeless lover, loved one, setting" (footnote, p. 385), and an early experiment with mythic retelling in the form of a dramatic monologue. Interestingly, of the other important Tennysonian dramatic monologues, only "The Lotos-Eaters" and "Tithonus" include extended visually oriented description. "St. Simeon Stylities," "Ulysses," and "Rizpah" include no word-painting at all, focusing, instead, on the depiction of the unique inner state of the speaker. "Ulysses" contains memorable flashes of visual imagery—for example, the lines, "to follow knowledge like a sinking star" (1. 31) or "The lights begin to twinkle from the rocks / The long day wanes: the slow moon climbs: the deep / Moans round with many voices" (11. 54–56). This suggestion of setting, enormously successful because so carefully selected and so rhythmically appropriate, is not allowed to flower into a fully developed description. This strategy maintains the focus upon the aged, stoical hero, Ulysses. Word-painting does not participate in this mythic retelling.

But it participates significantly in both "Oenone" and "The Lotos-Eaters." "Oenone" opens with a beautiful description by the nameless narrator of the vale of Ida, seen from a high perspective, another prospect vision, but here in classical, not Biblical context. The poem, Tennyson's first important classical idyll (defined as a little picture in verse) owes its form to Theocritus: opening setting, following by the love-lament of the abandoned nymph.

> There lies a vale in Ida, lovelier
> Than all the valleys of Ionian hills.
> The swimming vapour slopes athwart the glen,
> Puts forth an arm, and creeps from pine to pine,
> And loiters, slowly drawn. On either hand
> The lawns and meadow-ledges midway down
> Hang rich in flowers, and far below them roars
> The long brook falling through the cloven ravine
> In cataract after cataract to the sea.
> Behind the valley topmost Gargarus
> Stands up and takes the morning: but in front
> The gorges, opening wide apart, reveal
> Troas and Ilion's columned citadel,
> The crown of Troas.

(ll. 1–14)

Again, a dramatic landscape opens a narrative poem, but this word-painting is the most visually coherent we have yet examined. The coherence comes both from the underlying personification of the waters as a loitering spirit, and a clear organization reflective of how the eye progresses over a view. The landscape itself is unusually dramatic, and the passage vividly captures the valley of Cauteretz through which Tennyson and Hallam journeyed during the summer of 1830. Moving, falling water echoes and introduces active story telling. The mind's eye follows the descent of the water from glen to lawns and meadow-ledges to cloven ravine until it crashes into the sea far below. One can easily visualize the steps from high piney-glen downward "midway" where the flowers hang, and, finally, to the opening gorges through which one can glimpse Troy. This progression of the eye anticipates a similar movement in the poem from word-painting to narrative and from Oenone's isolation to her descent into the city to speak with Cassandra at the poem's end, a movement from nature to the human community.

Lush mountains which frame the realms of man represent peaceful harmony in the poem. Oenone, a nymph of Troy, is the daughter of Ida, and the nature imagery through the poem appropriately suggests her identity with the natural world. Word-painting, not limited to the opening prospect, suggests this identity at key points in the narrative of her betrayal by Paris. Fragments of vision that augment the opening word-painting here suggest a viewer sensitive to beauty, one who, in contrast with Mariana's fragmented vision, can put together the pieces of the external world in a coherent vision. Oenone notices, with unsentimental clarity:

> For now the noonday quiet holds the hill:
> The grasshopper is silent in the grass:
> The lizard, with his shadow on the stone,
> Rests like a shadow, and the winds are dead.
>
> (ll. 24–27)

Music sings in these assonant and rhythmical lines. They are appropriate to Oenone because she is the spirit of the Vale; and both her acute observation of tiny creatures and the way in which the shadow falls on the land to suggest the time of day convince us of her perfect sympathy with Nature. The gods come, bringing sorrow, but the pictures of her mountain home are the elements one retains from the poem. One such frozen picture, for example, presents Oenone, sitting solitarily as Paris approaches:

> Far-off the torrent called me from the cleft:
> Far off the solitary morning smote
> The streaks of virgin snow. With down-dropt eyes
> I sat alone: white-breasted like a star
> Fronting the dawn he moved:
>
> (ll. 53–57)

The passage evokes Oenone's vulnerability and innocence, as the one who will represent her doom approaches through a landscape whose spirit she represents.

A series of elaborate frames contains the story of the Judgment of Paris. First, the narrator describes the vale, and then Oenone describes the time before her fateful meeting with Paris, the Judgment of Paris itself, and the disaster to come. Like the knights who see the Holy Grail and are changed forever, Oenone cannot return to the peaceful life she lived before she saw Paris, and the poem ends with imagery of fire which replaces the water and earth of the opening description. A familiar mythic narrative amply supports the lusciousness of the natural descriptions in this poem. Word-painting, beautifully developed in "Oenone," adequately balances the elaboration of frames, the character of the speakers, and the clear narrative progression.

Similarly, in "The Lotos-Eaters," a landscape of gorgeous proportions which shares many features of the landscape in "Oenone" carries thematic meaning. Tennyson's descriptive opening stanzas in both poems derive from the same trip through the Pyrennees in 1830, but he uses them with opposite effect. "The Lotos-Eaters," far from placing us within an ongoing narrative, presents a mood very close to that of "Mariana," a state of lassitude and stasis which represents one of the trials of the *Odyssey* (ix, 82ff.). In the *Odyssey*, the mariners resist the death-lure of the Lotos-Eaters, but Tennyson chooses to dramatize those who fail to do so. The poet sets out to convince us by imagery and music that "slumber is more sweet than toil" (l. 171). Tennyson does so by what Langbaum calls, "an over-richness of landscape, imagery and . . . enervated cadence."[16]

In spite of the richness of its word-painting, this poem keeps landscape description distinctly secondary to the enactment of a state of being. By beginning the poem, not with his standard set piece, but, rather, with four lines of narrative, Tennyson indicates his awareness of the need for balance between narrative and descriptive materials in this mythic recounting.

> 'Courage!' he said, and pointed toward the land,
> 'This mounting wave will roll us shoreward soon.'
> In the afternoon they came unto a land
> In which it seemèd always afternoon.
> All round the coast the languid air did swoon,
> Breathing like one that hath a weary dream.
> Full-faced above the valley stood the moon;
> And, like a downward smoke, the slender stream
> Along the cliff to fall and pause and fall did seem.
>
> (ll. 1–9)

The opening lines, which thrust the reader into a story already in progress, establish the dominant motif of gently rolling movement and rhythm. The terms of the opening word-painting create an enervating sense of inertia which continues through the five Spenserian stanzas with which Tennyson introduces the eight-stanza Choric song of the becalmed mariners. Rolling waves, languid air, and a stuttering stream that appears to stop and start again as it descends the cliff substitute for "Oenone's" movement of descending waters.[17]

The second stanza reinforces the mood of becalming enchantment, with its repeating rhyme scheme of ababbcbcc and its long lines stretched out with the sounds of o and s.

> A land of streams! some, like a downward smoke,
> Slow-dropping veils of thinnest lawn, did go;
> And some through wavering lights and shadows broke,
> Rolling a slumbrous sheet of foam below.
> They saw the gleaming river seaward flow
> From the inner land; far off, three mountain-tops,
> Three silent pinnacles of agèd snow,
> Stood sunset-flushed: and, dewed with showery drops,
> Up-clomb the shadowy pine above the woven copse.
>
> (ll. 10–18)

The landscape, slow-moving and rolling gently, echoes the mood of the Lotos-Eaters themselves, who soon appear to lure the mariners toward the land, as the sun sets.

> The charmèd sunset lingered low adown
> In the red West: through mountain clefts the dale
> Was seen far inland, and the yellow down
> Bordered with palm, and many a winding vale
> And meadow, set with slender galingale;
> A land where all things always seemed the same!
> And round about the keel with faces pale,
> Dark faces pale against that rosy flame,
> The mild-eyed melancholy Lotos-eaters came.
>
> (ll. 19–27)

Nature conspires with the mood of the men to swerve the heroes from their path, in another thwarted quest pattern. In this poem, Tennyson uses word-painting to suggest the attraction of the sensual and the present, as opposed to the goal-oriented life of duty, toil, and death.

"Oenone" and "The Lotos-Eaters" exemplify mythic poems that successfully integrate word-painting with a coherent narrative. "The Palace of Art" proves instructive as an example of what happens to a poem's structure when gorgeous visually oriented pictures in the text overload a poem lacking a strong narrative substructure. Undoubtedly, Tennyson meant to provide a narrative structure, but it is buried in descriptive stanzas. "The Palace of Art" is very important as one of Tennyson's first experiments with the panel structure he was to use with great success in *In Memoriam,* but both 1832 and 1842 versions of the shorter poem demonstrate the pitfalls of overemphasizing word-painting. Unintentionally, the poem's structure gives a feeling of stasis equal to that of "The Lotos-Eaters." However, in the latter poem it is appropriate, whereas in the former it indicates a structural breakdown.

When the reader encounters "I built my soul a lordly pleasure-house" in the opening lines of "The Palace of Art," he may well expect a narrative poem to follow. But the poem actually describes the abode of a particular soul. The first two hundred lines lay out gardens, exterior, interior rooms with their pic-

tures and galleries, and central hall, decorated with busts of great men from
Dante to Milton and mosaics depicting the cycles of man's life. By the time
one hears again of the "she" in the poem, the reader may not be blamed for
having forgotten who "she" is! Having introduced the "soul" in the opening
lines, Tennyson fails to mention her in the sheer exuberance with which he details the descriptive panels of the "pleasure-house." When the poet returns to
the narrative material, he hurries through the recounting of the soul's hubris,
her subsequent fall, and her resolution to leave the palace for a simple cottage,
though she may one day return.

Clearly, Tennyson was more interested in word-paintings than in narrative
in "The Palace of Art." The subject of the poem partly justifies descriptive
technique here, for he enumerates an entire history of the arts in describing a
single architectural structure. But the last one-third of the poem must carry all
the narrative, and in such a way that it is possible to overlook the story line
altogether. The lack of balance between word-painting and narrative in this
work partly accounts for its structural weakness.

Even so, no examination of Tennyson's word-painting could ignore "The
Palace of Art." Individual stanzas present superb examples of Tennyson's verbal visualizations. Part II of the poem, for example, begins:

> Four courts I made, East, West and South and North,
>   In each a squared lawn, wherefrom
> The golden gorge of dragons spouted forth
>   A flood of fountain-foam.
>
> (ll. 21–24)

The section ends:

> Likewise the deep-set windows, stained and traced,
>   Would seem slow-flaming crimson fires
> From shadowed grots of arches interlaced,
>   And tipt with frost-like spires.
>
> (ll. 49–52)

These passages demonstrate Tennyson's mastery at using language to evoke the
object intensely seen. The integration of skillful word-paintings with a narrative
structure represents the chief remaining aesthetic challenge for Tennyson in his
mature period.

English Idylls and *The Princess:* Transitional Experiments

> Come down, O maid, from yonder mountain height:
> What pleasure lives in height (the shepherd sang)
> In height and cold, the splendour of the hills?
> But cease to move so near the Heavens, and cease

> To glide a sunbeam by the blasted Pine,
> To sit a star upon the sparkling spire;
> And come, for Love is of the valley, come,
> For Love is of the valley, come thou down
> And find him;
>
> *The Princess* (VII, ll. 177–85)

In addition to the important word-paintings we have just examined, *Poems* (1842) includes a number of visually oriented extended descriptions as part of a group of poems Tennyson calls *English Idylls*. These long, primarily narrative poems emphasize middle-class values and characters who perform their actions in the domesticated landscapes of the human community, rather than against the sublime mountain heights to which readers of Tennyson's early poetry have become accustomed. *English Idylls* show Tennyson turning away from the shorter metrical and structural experiments toward a successful long form that might combine narrative, lyric, and dramatic elements in a single work.

At least one of these *English Idylls,* however, concerns a mythic narrative to which Tennyson will return over and over throughout the rest of his life. It is, of course, "Morte d'Arthur," the early version of "The Passing of Arthur," which, with significant additions, constitutes the final book of *Idylls of the King*. The early version of this poem begins:

> So all day long the noise of battle rolled
> Among the mountains by the winter sea;
> Until King Arthur's table, man by man,
> Had fallen in Lyonnesse about their lord,
> King Arthur: then, because his wound was deep,
> The bold Sir Bedivere uplifted him,
> Sir Bedivere, the last of all his knights,
> And bore him to a chapel nigh the field,
> A broken chancel with a broken cross,
> That stood on a dark strait of barren land.
> On one side lay the Ocean, and on one
> Lay a great water, and the moon was full.
>
> (ll. 1–12)

A comparison between Tennyson's first word-paintings and the use of similar motifs in "Morte d'Arthur" indicates how the poet has learned to fuse description with a dramatic story in order to create verbal pictures that reflect the state of mind of the characters and that relate intimately to a now-dominant narrative. The lines above thrust the reader into a scene already in progress and describe a setting that is both convincingly real and a symbolic correlative to Arthur's fallen state.

Principles of contrast again lend compositional coherence to the description of landscape in which familiar Tennysonian motifs inhere. The barren land, chapel, and broken cross are symbolically appropriate to Arthur's last battle. Arthur lies in an isolated chapel standing between two great bodies of water under a full moon, and the drama of Bedivere's descent from and ascent to this high place occupies most of the action of the Idyll. Once again, Tennyson precisely locates elements in the imagined landscape setting (e.g. "on one side" and "on one"); and he also contrasts the dark strait and the full moon, the enclosed dark foreground and the ocean in moonlight, to dramatic advantage. In addition, enormous space lends poignance to Arthur lying wounded near the small chancel and the broken cross. All these elements indicate Tennyson's mastery of the language and technique of composing visually oriented description and relating it closely to narrative.

Later in "Morte d'Arthur," Sir Bedivere carries Arthur down to the lake where the funeral barge awaits him:

> But the other swiftly strode from ridge to ridge,
> Clothed with his breath, and looking, as he walked,
> Larger than human on the frozen hills.
> He heard the deep behind him, and a cry
> Before. His own thought drove him like a goad.
> Dry clashed his harness in the icy caves
> And barren chasms, and all to left and right
> The bare black cliff clanged round him, as he based
> His feet on juts of slippery crag that rang
> Sharp-smitten with the dint of armèd heels—
> And on a sudden, lo! the level lake,
> And the long glories of the winter moon.

(ll. 349–60)

The perspective for this memorable word-painting is Bedivere's; the reader sees and hears what he does, at this, the saddest moment of his life. But, at the same time, one observes Sir Bedivere as he descends from the frozen hills to the lake below. The scale of the figure contributes an important element to the impressiveness of the scene. He looks "larger than human," a proportion realized by the description of the way he strides from ridge to ridge like some god in a medieval illumination. As he moves through the dramatic landscape, with its frozen hills, its chasms, caves, cliffs, and crags, we move with him toward the stasis of the level place lying in the moonlight, and the dusky barge that waits below. Movement through contrasting levels of space provides a dramatic analogue to the anguish of the figure who bears his wounded king down toward death—or immortality.

As never before in Tennyson's word-paintings, this passage fuses the auditory with the visual. The dissonant sounds of cl, of explosive b's, d's and sibilant s's perfectly realize the inimical aspects of the landscape with its sharp, irregular shapes. Then, as if all of this provides a context for the peaceful scene, the harsh sounds give way to the incredibly gorgeous l's and o's, and the liquidity echoes the smooth, bright moonlit lake. This strategy appears to reverse Tennyson's technique in *The Devil and the Lady,* for here the scene itself is motionless and the lines leading up to the scene are full of activity.

The description from "Morte d'Arthur" contains several of the same visual motifs present in Tennyson's earliest word-paintings—light and darkness, cliff, mountain, lake, and moon seen in a prospect—but represents the perfected technique. Detail furthers dramatic action in "Morte d'Arthur" and suggests symbolic correspondences with the state of mind of the character and the climactic action. Later incorporated into "The Passing of Arthur," the release into moonlight prefigures the serene conclusion to the *Idylls* as a whole. Tennyson here severely tailors description to the needs of narrative, in contrast to his sometimes self-indulgent apprenticeship poetry.

Of Tennyson's other *English Idylls,* "The Gardener's Daughter" is most instructive for this history of Victorian word-painting, for it exemplifies the use of word-portraits in Tennyson's poetry. He organizes the narrative, subtitled "The Pictures," around a frozen, precisely visualized dramatic vignette, the moment when the narrator, an artist, first sees Rose, his beloved. As one learns from the poem's last moments, the speaker tells his story to an unidentified listener just before he unveils his painting of Rose as her lover first saw her. Thus, the form of the narrative returns us again and again to the moment in the story when the speaker first looks upon his beloved. The other picture, to which the subtitle refers, is one which his friend Eustace (Hallam?) paints of Juliet, his beloved, but this second picture is unimportant to the story.

A poem so pictorial in conception, which also includes an extended narrative, represents the next step in Tennyson's integration of word-painting with narrative. Culler postulates that the dominance of the novel after the 1820s partly accounts for Tennyson's interest in the idyll form in which several speakers' conversations about daily affairs enable him to include contemporary issues (p. 113). *English Idylls* and *The Princess* help Tennyson work out some techniques he later uses to combine description and narration in *Idylls of the King.*

In place of extended descriptions of sublime landscape, *English Idylls* offers word-paintings of domestic scenery and verbal tableaux. This shift rather neatly mirrors the parallel development in the middle novels of Charles Dickens. Novels of his middle period, such as *David Copperfield,* shift from an emphasis on picturesque word-painting to symbolic word-portraiture, and the subject of visually centered description becomes a frozen climactic moment described in painterly terms. Dickens, we recall, frames this description by some element that distances the viewer from a threatening emotion. The word-portrait in Tennyson's "The Gardener's Daughter" is less complicated than the word-portraits of Dickens, for it remains primarily at the pictorial level. Nevertheless, it employs a technique strikingly similar to the tableaux vivants of theatrical presentation which served as source for both Dickens and Tennyson.

Whereas in several early poems Tennyson locates women out of reach in towers ("The Lady of Shalott") or wastelands ("Mariana"), now he distances them in a frame, turning them into word-portraits controlled by the artist. One example from the early poetry shows how often Tennyson describes a beautiful woman in painterly terms. In a very early untitled sonnet, the poet paints a stylized picture of his beloved as if she had just stepped from an eighteenth-century hunting portrait.

> She took the dappled partridge fleckt with blood,
>   And in her hand the drooping pheasant bare,
>   And by his feet she held the woolly hare,
>   And like a master-painting where she stood,
> Lookt some new Goddess of an English wood.
>
> (ll. 1–5)

This sonnet, whose theme is how art "makes my love an Immortality," demonstrates Tennyson's familiarity with the conventions of portraiture when he attempts to mythologize a contemporary woman by putting her in the context of an established pictorial tradition.

In "The Gardener's Daughter," a tableau vivant forms the center of the poem and the narrative genesis for it. As Culler notes, "the essence of the tale lay not in the narrative, but in the picture which the narrator painted of Rose as she stood in her cottage door" (p. 117). Tennyson, who realized the importance of the word-portrait to his poem, remarked, "The centre of the poem, that passage describing the girl, must be full and rich. The poem is so, to a fault, especially the descriptions of nature, for the lover is an artist, but, this being so, the central picture must hold its place" (p. 508, headnote). Just as Oenone needed to convince us of her identity with the vale of Ida through the lushness of the word-painting, so the unnamed narrator must convince us of his adeptness as both artist and lover by the visual success of the central picture:

> For up the porch there grew an Eastern rose,
> That, flowering high, the last night's gale had caught,
> And blown across the walk. One arm aloft—
> Gowned in pure white, that fitted to the shape—
> Holding the bush, to fix it back, she stood,
> A single stream of all her soft brown hair
> Poured on one side: the shadow of the flowers
> Stole all the golden gloss, and, wavering
> Lovingly lower, trembled on her waist—
> Ah, happy shade—and still went wavering down,
> But, ere it touched a foot, that might have danced
> The greensward into greener circles, dipt,
> And mixed with shadows of the common ground!
> But the full day dwelt on her brows, and sunned
> Her violet eyes, and all her Hebe bloom,

And doubled his own warmth against her lips,
And on the bounteous wave of such a breast
As never pencil drew. Half light, half shade,
She stood, a sight to make an old man young.

(ll. 122–40)

Time provides the first frame for this word-portrait, for the narrator looks back on a moment long-past. In the verbal picture itself, the girl stands, framed by rose-bedecked porch, gracefully fixing the flower vine, her figure dramatically emphasized by a combination of light and shadow. The young men approach her through a rather picturesque landscape, moving from meadow to "one green wicket in a privet hedge," up the grassy walk with its pruned lilac to the garden, shaded by the dark-green cedar. All visual details are both vivid and precisely placed in the tableau. In a variation of the "Lo!" of prospect vision, Eustace urges the narrator, "Look! Look!" This picturesque vision centers on the human figure rather than the landscape. No wonder Culler calls these Idylls Tennyson's happiest poems, for they are suffused with the optimism of youth. When the narrator speaks to Rose, the frozen moment shatters, and she, granting his wish, presents him with a single rose, which symbolizes her gift of herself. But she does not speak, retaining the illusion of a picture come to life, and the narrator, "statue-like," becomes transfixed by the silent beauty of his vision.

The primary frame may be the past, but in a neat coherence between word-portraiture and narrative, the end of the poem returns us to the tableau vivant, here immortalized in the portrait the narrator has actually painted of his beloved. The poem ends with the speaker unveiling her portrait:

Behold her there,
As I beheld her ere she knew my heart,
My first, last love; the idol of my youth,
The darling of my manhood, and, alas!
Now the most blessèd memory of mine age.

(ll. 269–73)

Though time frames the portrait, the poem ends in the present with yet another view of the central moment of Love. Structurally, this poem does not begin with an extended word-painting that sets the scene. Instead, an extended visualization of the beloved forms the climactic moment of the narrative, its genesis, and its conclusion. There is no better example in all of Tennyson of the fusion of extended verbal visualization with narrative structure. Framed pictures of important figures in subsequent narrative poems illustrate the continuation of this motif, from the first picture of Princess Ida to the lawn party in *In Memoriam,* to Guinevere and Lancelot framed in the high windows at Camelot. All these word-portraits expand upon the essential new use of visually oriented description first exploited in "The Gardener's Daughter." In some cases, these word-portraits, simple visual motifs in the early Idyll, become more organically fused with both the narrative and the symbolic meaning of later long poetry. They thereby come to represent both a visual image and the thought held within it which is a fourth kind of descriptive poetry.

The Princess: A Medley (1847), a fascinating, failed poem, contains too many unfused materials and lacks a consistent and appropriate tone. Both textual and biographical commentary indicate that Tennyson recognized problems in this poem which he revised more fully than any of his long works. Its formal problems continued to disturb the poet twenty-two years after its publication. In 1869, Frederick Locker-Lampson tells us that Tennyson "talked of *The Princess* with something of regret, of its fine blank verse and the many good things in it: 'but,' said he, 'though truly original, it is after all, only a medley'" (Ricks headnote, p. 743).

The denigration of the form of *The Princess* is curiously defensive, considering that Tennyson eagerly attacks problems of form and genre in the longer poems he began publishing in the late 1840s. In *The Princess* (1847), *In Memoriam* (1850), *Maud* (1855), and *Idylls of the King* (1842–74), Tennyson explores problems of narrative form in poetry. Visually oriented description shifts to accommodate new emphases in the poetry. This subject will occupy the rest of my study.

The Princess represents Tennyson's most extensive experiment to that time in combining dramatic, lyric, and narrative materials in a coherent work. Its dramatic premise—the "tale told from mouth to mouth"—justifies a structure in seven parts told by seven speakers. The young women in the party of friends contribute occasional lyrics that divide the narrative. Thus, the shape of the narrative emphasizes a medley or miscellany form and negates the need for a single speaker or point of view. But here Tennyson outfoxed himself because the poem never manages to differentiate one speaker from another, and the voice we hear (Tennyson's, thinly disguised) never quite decides on a suitable tone. The men want a story "mock-heroic gigantesque," but the women request a serious tale, "true-heroic—true-sublime." So, the speaker finally admits that, in an attempt to please both men ("mockers") and women ("realists"), by finding a "middle way,"

> I moved as in a strange diagonal,
> And maybe neither pleased myself nor them.
>
> (Conclusion, ll. 27–28)

Ultimately, less than perfect though it is, *The Princess* offers an important example of the next step in the development of Tennyson's word-painting. As Priestley explains, Tennyson's early poetry experiments with heroic, elegaic, idyllic, pictorially romantic, satiric, reflective, pastoral, exotic, and other effects.[18] *The Princess* includes all these elements and more, in somewhat uneasy juxtaposition. Robert B. Martin, speaking of this work, comments, "It showed baldly his fundamental problem of believing that basically disparate material could be fused if they had enough connective."[19] The segmented structure of the poem suggests an increasingly popular Tennysonian strategy. Breaking a narrative or long poem into distinct parts gives the poet the flexibility of form and the suggestiveness of significant juxtaposition that he was to use even more successfully in *In Memoriam* and *Idylls of the King*.

The Princess offers Tennyson a chance to experiment with fairy-tale motifs, the theme of shadow and substance, the quality of "weird seizures" in a main character, and combinations of blank-verse drama, gorgeous lyrics, and some descriptive materials. Elements from this early "mine" will reappear, re-worked to greater advantage, in later long poems. *In Memoriam,* for example, focuses on a structure of linked lyrics, and *Idylls of the King,* which explores narrative without the pretense of a unifying speaker, instead frames the story with Arthur's dream and lets each idyll speak for itself.

Much as *The Princess* looks ahead to later works of Tennyson, it also looks back to the *English Idylls,* with their emphasis on comforting, and some-times sentimentalized, relations within the human community. Sublime nature gives way to a domesticated landscape in *The Princess;* and the relationship be-tween man and nature is by way of nature tamed as we saw in "The Gardener's Daughter." The lyric, "Come Down, O maid" (see the epigraph to this chapter) admirably suggests this shift in interest from the isolated woman to the con-structive community participant.

Visually oriented description of any significant length hardly appears in *The Princess,* yet the few word-paintings we do have are crucial to the narra-tive because they focus several of its most significant themes, reflect the form of the "medley" and frame and contain the narrative. Thus, while they are not the centers of the story, they represent a sophistication in Tennyson's use of word-painting and word-portraiture as part of a long poem.

The story of *The Princess* is fairly simple to summarize but rather more complicated to tell. The speaker attends a country picnic given by the father of his college friend, Walter, on the grounds of his large estate. At the party are a group of young friends of Walter and his sister Lilia, Sir Walter's tenants, and members of the Mechanic's Institute. In the course of the afternoon, the young people agree to tell an impromptu tale on the subject of women's rights. Between this prologue and a short conclusion lie seven sections that recount the story of Princess Ida, a fierce intellectual who establishes a college for women from which men are banished. The action of the story concerns the attempts of the Prince, to whom Ida has been betrothed in childhood, to win her back. Dis-guised with several friends as women, the Prince infiltrates the college and, when exposed, receives a serious wound in battle with Ida's brother. Nursed back to health by the victorious Ida, he ultimately wins her over by his helplessness. In the uneasy resolution to the poem, Tennyson means to suggest that a successful marriage must rest on equality between the sexes. A solution close to the advocacy of androgeny emerges when the Princess loses her "masculine" qualities, turning from the life of the mind to the occupation of nurse, and the Prince proves in battle that he is no coward.

This long poem confines word-painting to the prologue and conclusion which frame the story of Princess Ida. Both parts of the frame contain extended descriptive passages, though Tennyson had trouble with these sections, too. Locker-Lampson reports that Tennyson told him "that it was very difficult in blank verse to give descriptions . . . and at the same time to retain poetical elevation. Tennyson insisted that the employment of rhyme would have made it much easier" (Ricks, headnote, p. 743). It is true that these word-paintings are fairly uninteresting, especially when compared to the glorious visual imagery of the more inspired erotic lyrics within the poem such as "Tears, Idle Tears" or "Now Sleeps the Crimson Petal." These lyrics do not qualify as word-paintings because they do not employ a coherent visual organization.

Tennyson uses descriptions of place to set an old story in a contemporary context, as has been his habit. He introduces the poem with an extended description of the setting for Sir Walter's picnic. First, the speaker tours the major house with his friend, Walter, and then he describes the scene on the lawn. These passages, taken together, give an impression of a vast "jumble" of elements from the worlds of science, ancient history and human endeavor.

> and on the pavement lay
> Carved stones of the Abbey-ruin in the park,
> Huge Ammonites, and the first bones of Time;
> And on the tables every clime and age
> Jumbled together; celts and calumets,
> Claymore and showshoe, toys in lava, fans
> Of sandal, amber, ancient rosaries,
> Laborious orient ivory sphere in sphere.
>
> (ll. 13–20)

What a wonderful Victorian jumble it is, augmented, in subsequent lines—too many to quote here—by Sir Walter's ancestral armor and arms! Walter calls the speaker back to the present with a walk through the park. Along the way, one sees another jumble, this time the fruits of recent scientific discovery, among which the guests cavort:

> There moved the multitude, a thousand heads:
> The patient leaders of their Institute
> Taught them with facts. One reared a font of stone
> And drew, from butts of water on the slope,
> The fountain of the moment, playing, now
> A twisted snake, and now a rain of pearls,
> Or steep-up spout whereon the gilded ball
> Danced like a wisp: and somewhat lower down

A man with knobs and wires and vials fired
A cannon: Echo answered in her sleep
From hollow fields: and here were telescopes
For azure views; and there a group of girls
In circle waited, whom the electric shock
Dislinked with shrieks and laughter:

(Prologue, ll. 57–70)

The verse-sentence, going on for another twenty lines, describes the paddlers on the lake, the toy railroad that jets steam about the knolls, and the fire-balloon that rises to drop a parachute. In addition, a telegraph flashes messages and, elsewhere in the park, some frivolous nonlearners play croquet, babies roll in the grass, and men and women dance country dances to the accompaniment of a violin.

Like the speaker, we too are soon "satiated," and the retreat to the Gothic ruins of the Abbey, which protect the narrator from present chaos, represents a welcome relief. But why does the poet include two long catalogues of seemingly miscellaneous visual elements? First, the description functions as Tennyson's other introductory visually oriented descriptions of setting have done to create the context for narration. In addition, the poet has found a way to include recent scientific experiments in the frame of a poem ostensibly about the past, thus capturing the attention of the contemporary reader. But notice how little detail we have concerning any one feature either of manor house or of the activities outside. What is intended is a mere survey of elements in this landscape, named but not described with much specificity. The description of the park illuminates a contemporary "prospect" and its subject matter is appropriate to the idyll form, awash with reflections of middle-class and upper-class customs and concerns. The word-painting also sets the tone for the medley. For what are both opening descriptions if not "medleys," collections of data swept by the speaker's eye from foreground to background and from ground level to heavens and back to earth?

The opening description also suggests the didactic nature of *The Princess*. At the picnic, teachers of the Mechanic's Institute instruct their students by means of scientific demonstrations, much as Princess Ida, Psyche, and Lady Blanche will teach their students about the latest geological and scientific discoveries at their woman's college. And, along the way, the Prince and his friends will gain information about the lectures they infiltrate in disguise, and all involved will learn the proper balance between the sexes by the end of the poem.

The opening word-paintings, then, set the dominant methodology for the "medley" and suggest important thematic motifs. They also provide the appropriate frame of the present within which to enclose a fairy tale with contemporary relevance. Certainly, Tennyson wished to defuse the controversial subject of women's rights through the device of the frame, and word-painting gives him a way to contain the past within the present. There is no room in the opening word-painting for the sort of sublime landscape we have noted in earlier poems, but, rather, the scene may remind one of a Brueghel-like profusion of visual vignettes without the grotesquerie.

Another set of two visually organized word-paintings balances these introductory word-paintings by way of conclusion, although both sets are embedded in other narrative and didactic lines. Many have found the conclusion to this massive poem to be "inconclusive." Tennyson uses two significant passages of description to close the frame opened by the Prologue. Looking out again at the scene of the morning's activity, the speaker achieves a momentary prospect vision, one from which feverish activity has been erased, and the beautiful rustic landscape returns to inspire.

> we climbed
> The slope to Vivian-place, and turning saw
> The happy valleys, half in light, and half
> Far-shadowing from the west, a land of peace;
> Gray halls alone among their massive groves;
> Trim hamlets; here and there a rustic tower
> Half-lost in belts of hop and breadths of wheat;
> The shimmering glimpses of a stream; the seas;
> A red sail, or a white; and far beyond,
> Imagined more than seen, the skirts of France.
>
> (Conclusion, ll. 40–48)

An impressionistic rendering of many of the same visual motifs we have traced through Tennyson's word-paintings reappear here. The physical prospect serves here, though, as catalyst to a political vision of the moderate way toward change that the speaker prefers to the more violent revolutions of the France that he can just barely see in the distance. The landscape lies in dramatic half-light, suggestive of a peace descending on a busy scene. It also suggests the happy outcome of the story of Princess Ida and the Prince, who have also found a middle way between the extremes of feminism and male chauvinism. This survey of the landscape coheres, reflecting the perspective of the viewer, who finishes the day and the story well-pleased with its conclusions. It suggests a visionary moment in which the speaker can glimpse a better social and political entity emerging from present chaos, a future time to balance past and present.

Tennyson sets beside the description of the prospect a second visually oriented passage, this one a word-portrait of Sir Walter bidding farewell to his guests and tenants who cheer for him as the sun goes down on a happy day of festivities. Sir Walter's word-portrait stands as a kind of image of Olde England, and his figure symbolizes stability, fertility, harmony with the land and protection for his dependents, and responsibility—qualities that combine both physical strength and intellectual forcefulness.

In such discourse we gained the garden rails,
And there we saw Sir Walter where he stood,
Before a tower of crimson holly-hoaks,
Among six boys, head under head, and looked
No little lily-handed Baronet he,
A great broad-shouldered genial Englishman,
A lord of fat prize-oxen and of sheep,
A raiser of huge melons and of pine,
A patron of some thirty charities,
A pamphleteer on guano and on grain,
A quarter-sessions chairman, abler none;
Fair-haired and redder than a windy morn;

(Conclusion, ll. 80–91)

The picture of Sir Walter gives one a medley of qualities, this time a salute to the archetypal country gentleman, the backbone of England's social rural stability which emphasizes the proper mix of positive qualities.

The final descriptive passages to be discussed here reinforce the basic structural principle of the medley by giving, in several set pieces, fragments of an implied resolution to the poem. Balance restored, the reader returns to the present—where the speaker suggests a moderate rhythm for social and political change—and, as Culler so neatly notes, a variegated landscape echoes the view that life itself is a medley (p. 145)!

That descriptive materials are concentrated in the frame of Prologue and Conclusion is, in my opinion, no coincidence, and demonstrates Tennyson's awareness of the need for a frame to control the disparate content and form of the poem itself. Within the story of Princess Ida, there are no extended visually oriented landscape descriptions at all. Even when Ida and the Prince, galloping out on a geology field trip, survey the scene below, prospect is suppressed in favor of didactic narrative:

And up we came to where the river sloped
To plunge in cataract, shattering on black blocks
A breadth of thunder. O'er it shook the woods,
And danced the colour, and, below, stuck out
The bones of some vast bulk that lived and roared
Before man was. She gazed awhile and said,
'As these rude bones to us, are we to her
That will be.'

(III, ll. 273–80)

Instead of sublime word-painting, one hears about "black blocks," in the language of science. But the observation is neither precisely descriptive nor is it inspired poetry. Its tone is heavily didactic, as is the lesson Ida extracts from the animal remains they observe. The Princess herself eschews poetic things, preferring hard, cold facts, and the Prince obliges her by curbing his own eloquent side.

But the Prince allows his real feelings to emerge as he first describes Ida in a verbal portrait that suggests the tableaux vivants we have already noted in the *English Idylls*. The elevated diction of the Prince's descriptions presents a tonal problem for the reader, for Ida's attire and pose are so exaggerated that it is hard to know if one ought to laugh at her pretentiousness or to revere her heroic posture.

> There at a board by tome and paper sat,
> With two tame leopards couched beside her throne,
> All beauty compassed in a female form.
> The Princess; liker to the inhabitant
> Of some clear planet close upon the Sun,
> Than our man's earth; such eyes were in her head,
> And so much grace and power, breathing down
> From over her arched brows, with every turn
> Lived through her to the tips of her long hands,
> And to her feet.
>
> (II, ll. 18–27)

The unfortunate word order and the mixing of metaphor give the reader no clear picture of this ruler. Is her nose above her brow, that she should "breathe down" grace and power? But the intention to glorify the Princess with a frozen word-portrait is clear. The inadequacy of the language here points to a continual weakness in the poem concerning characterization.

For all its imperfections, however, *The Princess* illustrates Tennyson's use of word-painting and word-portraiture to place narrative materials in a descriptive context. His interests have been drawn away from extended description and toward extended narratives by the time he wrote *The Princess*. The few verbal visualizations in the poem occur at important points in the structure and fulfill significant functions in relation to the narrative. The next step in the development of Tennyson's word-painting echoes a similar development in Dickens's late novels as the poet moves toward more symbolic description in *In Memoriam* and *Idylls of the King*.

In Memoriam and *Idylls of the King:* **Compensatory Visions for Loss**

> Thereat once more he moved about, and clomb
> Even to the highest he could climb, and saw,
> Straining his eyes beneath an arch of hand,
> Or thought he saw, the speck that bare the King,
> Down that long water opening on the deep
> Somewhere far off, pass on and on, and go
> From less to less and vanish into light.
> And the new sun rose bringing the new year.
>
> *Idylls of the King* (ll. 462–end)

Tennyson's early poetry documents his heavy dependence on the eighteenth-century and Romantic traditions in poetry, represented in the present study by Thomson and Wordsworth. In works of Tennyson's "middle" period, represented here by the dramatic monologues, *English Idylls,* and *The Princess,* Tennyson occasionally uses word-paintings to set a scene ("Oenone" and "The Lotos-Eaters"), to catch a mood ("Mariana"), or to frame a narrative (*The Princess*).

Tennyson uses word-painting somewhat differently in *In Memoriam.* In this poem, Tennyson experiments with ways to fuse a series of what T. S. Eliot has called "linked lyrics" by using recurrent imagery. *In Memoriam* uses all four kinds of visually oriented poetic description. Most frequently, Tennyson employs simple visual images, appropriate to brief lyrics, in order to make the reader feel the grieving poet's mental state. These images usually illuminate both object and viewer. Tennyson also reiterates a series of natural objects that eventually achieve the status of symbol, such as the yew, the oak, and the sycamore. Lastly, the poet often springs from visually oriented passages to visionary experiences, as in the famous description of the lawns at Somersby which precedes the visionary climax of the poetic sequence (lyric 95).

With the exception of the Somersby scene, none of this visually oriented material represents a coherent word-painting. Instead, Tennyson fragments his word-paintings in order to construct visually oriented poetry whose sensory data contribute to the gradual accretion of meaning in the poem. The speaker moves from grief and doubt to hope and renewed faith in the implied narrative of the soul's progress that lies beneath the ordering of lyrics. Significantly, the only extended natural description occurs in the climactic lyric 95, "By night we linger'd on the lawn." Tennyson uses this beautiful natural setting in a way similar to Wordsworth's use of the sublime landscapes of the Simplon Pass and Mount Snowdon—to precede a visionary moment that, paradoxically, cancels the senses in a moment that transcends earth and time.

But whereas Tennyson rarely uses word-painting as such in *In Memoriam,* his description of natural elements is highly significant, as is the placement of fragments of external nature and coherent description. A. C. Bradley explains Tennyson's division of the poem into four sections and the reader notes a corresponding infrequency of extended description in the first half of the poem.[20]

In the first section dark imagery prevails, and noise cancels peace and harmony, helping to articulate the despairing mood of the speaker. In the second section nature also fails to comfort and redeem man. In these two sections— roughly, the first half of the poem—it is significant that the speaker, like Mariana, cannot form the elements of the outer world into a coherent landscape. Consumed with grief and depression, he incorporates intensely seen fragments into his verses, but cannot compose them into a unity which assumes a consistent perspective.

Although one suspects a deliberate suppression of word-painting in the first half of the poem, Lyric 38 corroborates that this suppression is employed as a deliberate poetic strategy. In the first Spring of the poet's loss, Tennyson writes:

> With weary steps I loiter on,
>   Though always under alter'd skies
>   The purple from the distance dies,
> My prospect and horizon gone.
>
> (XXXVIII, ll. 1–4)

The poet cannot grasp the necessary perspective for a picturesque or sublime word-painting because he cannot see anything outside himself. He finds "a doubtful gleam of solace" in the auditory sense that usually accompanies the visual in Tennyson's word-paintings, however, for he finds he still can sing (write his poems), though he cannot find joy in springtime.

The suppression of visually oriented passages in the first section of the poem joins with the nightmare visions of the second section to offer a compelling picture of the isolation of grief and the estrangement of the poet from the natural world. In the most stunning visually oriented imagery of the first half of the sequence, Tennyson conveys the terrors of the night for a soul in torment, cut off from both his soulmate and from nature and God:

> I cannot see the features right,
>   When on the gloom I strive to paint
>   The face I know; the hues are faint
> And mix with hollow masks of night;
>
> Cloud-towers by ghostly masons wrought,
>   A gulf that ever shuts and gapes,
>   A hand that points, and pallèd shapes
> In shadowy thoroughfares of thought;
>
> And crowds that stream from yawning doors,
>   And shoals of pucker'd faces drive;
>   Dark bulks that tumble half alive,
> And lazy lengths on boundless shores;
>
> Till all at once beyond the will
>   I hear a wizard music roll,
>   And through a lattice on the soul
> Looks thy fair face and makes it still.
>
> (LXX)

This lyric employs a technique similar to the technique used in "The Kraken" simultaneously to suggest precisely focused sensory data and amorphousness. The lack of clear causality mirrors the phenomena of dreams. When the poet tries to recall the face of the beloved lost one, it will not come clear. He cannot "paint" it because he cannot compose its distinctness against the background of the night. Instead, the face merges with night shadows, and alarmingly fades, replaced by clouds, chasms, the enigmatic hand that points, and "palled shapes." Frenzy and languor confusedly mix in the third stanza in imagery surely borrowed later by T. S. Eliot for his images of London. Yet, suddenly, the visual terrors of this lyric give way to a vision of the fair face of the beloved that stills the strange "wizard music," and perhaps the soul as well (the "it" of the last line refers both to the terrifyingly confused scene and the state of the soul). The lyric prefigures the climactic moment in lyric 95 when the spirit of Hallam returns in a visionary communion with the poet.

The nightmare represents the most frightening visual correlative to the poet's internal state, painted by his subconscious as an image of torment. It is the clearest use of visually oriented images to suggest the nadir of the poet's despair in *In Memoriam*. At the same time, the last stanza looks ahead to the possibility of composure and to reconciliation in the future.

It seems to be more than mere coincidence that the lyric immediately following lyric 70 offers another hint of the rebirth of hope and that its vehicle is another reference to that seminal trip that Tennyson and Hallam took in the summer of 1830 whose vistas form the inspiration for the word-paintings in "Oenone" and "The Lotos-Eaters." The last stanza of lyric 71 returns us to the "Present of the Past," as Tennyson calls it; and for the first time in *In Memoriam* the poet describes sublime mountain scenery in a brief visual survey:

> Beside the river's wooded reach,
>   The fortress, and the mountain ridge,
>   The cataract flashing from the bridge,
> The breaker breaking on the beach.
>
> (LXXI, ll. 13–16)

This turn from present despair to past joys signals the incipient change in the poem from isolation, sterility, and estrangement to one of involvement with a landscape of springtime, an awareness of the natural world, and an openness to connections with other human beings. By including references to natural elements along with thoughts of the present and future, the poet indicates that the period of most acute mourning is coming to an end. The idea is made explicit in the temporal structure of the lyrics by the break in chronology after lyric 71 to announce the first anniversary of Hallam's death.

Significantly, longer, more descriptive, more narrative—in general, more discursive—poems compose the second half of the sequence (lyrics 78–131). The form of the poems echoes the growing psychic strength of the speaker that enables him to sustain a longer poetic statement. Perhaps the lengthening form of lyrics also correlates with the turning from emotions of grief—more appropriate to brief lyrics—to the intellectual problems of faith that concern the poet in the last two sections of the poem. Beginning with lyric 85, the poet increasingly turns his attention to the phenomenological world as expressive of his growing faith in the spirit and the human community.

The prefiguring of a shift in the poet's frame of mind around lyric 85 (the poem addressed to Edmund Lushington) emerges from a close study of visually oriented passages in *In Memoriam*. The narrative of the soul's progress from doubt and despair to faith and reconciliation nicely correlates with the use of word-painting in the sequence and shows how Tennyson's word-paintings absorb narrative and dramatic intent in this work. For example, a second spring song (lyric 83) gives us the first touch of specific color and carefully observed natural phenomena in the sequence.

> Bring orchis, bring the foxglove spire,
>   The little speedwell's darling blue,
>   Deep tulips dashed with fiery dew,
> Laburnums, dropping-wells of fire.
>
> (LXXXIII, ll. 9–12)

Invoking spring to quicken the poet's song, the minute observation and carefully composed coloration of this stanza fall upon the reader's imagination with the effect of water after drought, for vivid colorful detail has been inappropriate to the grief registered in the first half of the sequence. Compare this stanza, for example, to those from the first spring song (lyric 38), which held "neither prospect nor horizon" for the grieving poet. Lyric 83 suggests that the speaker can begin to see the natural world again, and to allow it to comfort him.

The lyrics that follow expand upon the "low beginnings of content" noted in lyric 84. Lyrics from 85 through 94 are full of sense impressions of springtime that testify to the poet's rebirth along with the land's. Lyrics 85–90 dramatize "nascent hope" in an additive structure of lyrics that, while not really word-painting, nevertheless resembles an extended visually oriented description. These five lyrics, and the four that follow invoking Hallam's spirit to return, set the scene for the climactic moment in the sequence, lyric 95. Taken together, these nine lyrics represent the most lush visual poetry of the entire sequence and make the last section (lyrics 104–31) seem dry by comparison.

Lyric 85 begins as the poet addresses Edmund Lushington who is soon to be his brother-in-law. The poet seeks brotherhood with his new friend, and, in the last stanza, offers him the gift of the late primrose, which resembles, though is not identical to, the flowers of Spring. He wishes for a "late" friendship that might echo, though never really equal, his youthful friendship with Hallam. As if the act of trusting once again releases the poet from his self-imprisonment, this attempt at connection with another is immediately followed by the first extended visually oriented lyric in the series. Following soon after the lyric invoking spring (83), lyric 85 praises nature; and lyric 86 achieves a prospect vision at last:

Sweet after showers, ambrosial air,
>   That rollest from the gorgeous gloom
>   Of evening over brake and bloom
And meadow, slowly breathing bare

The round of space, and rapt below
>   Through all the dewy-tasselled wood,
>   And shadowing down the hornèd flood
In ripples, fan my brows and blow

The fever from my cheek, and sigh
>   The full new life that feeds thy breath
>   Throughout my frame, till Doubt and Death,
Ill brethren, let the fancy fly

From belt to belt of crimson seas
>   On leagues of odour streaming far,
>   To where in yonder orient star
A hundred spirits whisper 'Peace.'

(LXXXVI)

Sweet-smelling air following spring rain rolls over the wide spaces of meadow, wood, and infinite space, and comes to heal the poet of his feverish doubts. In a wonderful cinematic movement, the air activates heights, then descends to meadows, and finally reaches the poet who stands in the landscape. It then heals him with the breath of life, and dismisses the allegorical figures, Doubt and Death, who have been omnipresent to this point. Once they are banished, the poet receives the first expansive spatial vision in *In Memoriam* as he looks to the evening star, and the auditory sense reinforces sight and touch, whispering, "Peace." Suffering and Nature's healing touch have earned the poet this vision of the unity between language, breath, poetry, and Hallam.[21] In lyric 86 these four elements finally merge.

Two further word-paintings augment this prospect vision that testifies to the psychological healing of the speaker. In lyric 87 the poet returns to walk the streets of Cambridge and to revisit sites where he lived with Hallam. This time he can remember the happy times they had, no longer needing to repress all memory of his friend. And, in lyric 89, he paints the first of two pictures of the lawn at Somersby. To "ambrosial air" the poet adds "ambrosial dark." The long lyric begins:

Witch-elms that counterchange the floor
>   Of this flat lawn with dusk and bright;
>   And thou, with all thy breadth and height
Of foliage, towering sycamore;

(LXXXIX, ll. 1–4)

Tennyson invokes the scene at Somersby with a few, well selected details. One can easily picture "the landscape winking thro' the heat" and hear the summer sounds of scythe and warm winds that knock the pears from the trees. Here, Hallam and Tennyson spent "golden" afternoons with Tennyson's sister, and discussed Socrates and the advantages of living in town or country. Now the poet can bear to recall vividly the last scenes of their friendship in a kind of tableau vivant of memory:

> We talked: the stream beneath us ran,
> The wine-flask lying couched in moss,
>
> Or cooled within the glooming wave;
> And last, returning from afar,
> Before the crimson-circled star
> Had fallen into her father's grave,
>
> And brushing ankle-deep in flowers,
> We heard behind the woodbine veil
> The milk that bubbled in the pail,
> And buzzings of the honied hours.
>
> (LXXXIX, ll. 43–52)

Sound, taste and sight operate together in this passage to produce a vivid recollection of the past and prepare us for the second important episode on this same lawn in the present, the spiritual return of Hallam.

Most commentators agree that lyric 95 is the climax of *In Memoriam*, marking the turn from doubt to certainty concerning the soul's immortality with the recovery of Hallam's soul from the land of the dead. The present study of visually oriented passages in the sequence reveals how these sections contribute to the reader's sense that the poet is now in a frame of mind receptive to spiritual or visionary insight. We have seen this quickening in the imagery itself, which has turned from winter, or negation of sense impressions, to spring and acceptance of the evidence of the senses. Ultimately doubting the illusions of sight, the poet requests a tactile sign. Word-painting sets the mood for such an event.

The visually oriented sections of lyric 95 frame and contain the essentially nonvisual climactic moment in the sequence, moving from nightfall to daybreak. Significantly, silence and sightlessness attend the culminating moment. The poem neatly divides into four stanzas of scene-setting, eight stanzas of the mystical moment itself, and four final stanzas to close the frame.

The first four stanzas compose the most fully realized word-painting in *In Memoriam*.

> By night we lingered on the lawn,
> For underfoot the herb was dry;
> And genial warmth; and o'er the sky
> The silvery haze of summer drawn;
>
> And calm that let the tapers burn
> Unwavering: not a cricket chirr'd:

> The brook alone far-off was heard,
> And on the board the fluttering urn:
>
> And bats went round in fragrant skies,
> And wheeled or lit the filmy shapes
> That haunt the dusk, with ermine capes
> And woolly breasts and beaded eyes;
>
> While now we sang old songs that pealed
> From knoll to knoll, where, couched at ease,
> The white kine glimmered, and the trees
> Laid their dark arms about the field.

(XCV, ll. 1–16)

The speaker's ability to compose a coherent verbal picture of the landscape in which he stands testifies to a soul at peace, one ready for the next desired plateau of spiritual experience. Sounds are muted, and the air is still, sweetly perfumed with summer odors. Wonderfully precise visual touches show the poet's delight in natural phenomena (see stanza 3, e.g.). Nature is in harmony with the happy group of folk who linger on the lawn singing old songs, and the trees seem to embrace the field. A mood of peaceful expectancy evoked by specificity of detail indicates a suspenseful moment different in kind from any other in *In Memoriam*. Word-painting helps prepare the way for a climactic event.

The moment when Hallam's spirit "flashes" upon the poet's soul goes beyond both language and sight but rests in tactile authentication, if only for the moment itself. Once the mystical trance passes, the Somersby lawn returns, and significant elements of the opening frame combine to enclose a timeless, climactic moment, restoring "normal" vision and recommencing normal life.

> Till now the doubtful dusk revealed
> The knolls once more where, couched at ease,
> The white kine glimmered, and the trees
> Laid their dark arms about the field:
>
> And sucked from out the distant gloom
> A breeze began to tremble o'er
> The large leaves of the sycamore,
> And fluctuate all the still perfume,
>
> And gathering freshlier overhead,
> Rocked the full-foliaged elms, and swung
> The heavy-folded rose, and flung
> The lilies to and fro, and said,
>
> 'The dawn, the dawn,' and died away;
> And East and West, without a breath,
> Mixt their dim lights, like life and death,
> To broaden into boundless day.

(XCV, ll. 49–64)

The first stanza of the concluding four repeats the description of kine and trees; and, as if to announce the end to the experience, the blowing breeze replaces the stillness, announcing the dawn in an image even more full of hope than the concluding image of *Idylls of the King* with which this section of my discussion began. In both poems, word-painting frames a climactic moment.

Visually oriented description falters after this climactic passage from *In Memoriam*, as do the tightness of the implied narrative of the soul's progress and the integration of the two. In a group of three lyrics, for example, the poet bids farewell to Somersby (lyrics 100–103), but the landscape he describes gives us very little in the way of a precise vision of the present scene. Rather, the poet is already thinking of how his lands will look in the future, "unwatched, unloved, uncared for." Lyric 103 closes this group of poems with another dream vision, this one an allegory in which life is pictured as a progress down a river to the sea which stands for eternity. The downward movement converts the incipient journey motif of earlier sections into an optimistic interpretation of the poet's place in history.

The fourth section (lyrics 104–31) contains only three visually oriented passages worthy of attention here. Lyric 119 describes the poet's return to Hallam's house on Wimpole Street.

> Doors, where my heart was used to beat
> So quickly, not as one that weeps
> I come once more; the city sleeps;
> I smell the meadow in the street;
>
> I hear a chirp of birds; I see
> Betwixt the black fronts long-withdrawn
> A light-blue lane of early dawn,
> And think of early days and thee,
>
> And bless thee, for thy lips are bland,
> And bright the friendship of thine eye;
> And in my thoughts with scarce a sigh
> I take the pressure of thine hand.
>
> (CXIX)

In contrast to the first lyric describing the same scene (lyric 7: "Dark house, by which once more I stand"), the poet demonstrates his ability to connect with nature, man, and memory. He can smell, hear, and see the beauties of nature once more; he is cured of his earlier despair. He now knows that in some sense Hallam is not lost to him; the taking of the pressure of his hand resolves the hand motif that runs through the sequence and provides a second moment of communion to put beside the climactic one at Somersby.

Two further visually oriented passages from *In Memoriam* offer images that crystallize some of Tennyson's thoughts concerning contemporary scientific discoveries and visions of apocalypse. They are cinematic in effect, but they do not connect organically with the narrative of the soul's progress we have been following in the present discussion, nor are they developed elaborately enough to qualify as word-paintings. Lyric 123 describes a visionary moment:

> There rolls the deep where grew the tree.
> O earth, what changes hast thou seen!
> There where the long street roars, hath been
> The stillness of the central sea.
>
> The hills are shadows, and they flow
> From form to form, and nothing stands;
> They melt like mist, the solid lands,
> Like clouds they shape themselves and go.
>
> But in my spirit will I dwell,
> And dream my dream, and hold it true;
> For though my lips may breathe adieu,
> I cannot think the thing farewell.
>
> (CXXIII)

The second stanza dramatizes the evolution of the shapes of mountains in an effective kinetic image. And, several lyrics later, the poet presents an even more powerful image, this one a terrifying depiction of the vengeance to befall those who do not heed the divine call for social truth and justice:

> They tremble, the sustaining crags;
> The spires of ice are toppled down,
>
> And molten up, and roar in flood;
> The fortress crashes from on high,
> The brute earth lightens to the sky,
> And the great Æon sinks in blood,
>
> And compassed by the fires of Hell,
> While thou, dear spirit, happy star,
> O'erlook'st the tumult from afar,
> And smilest, knowing all is well.
>
> (CXXVII, ll. 11–20)

Such passages pepper the last section of the sequence and lend the section weight and flavor. But they do not relate to the narrative of the soul's progress that we have been following.

The prologue and epilogue to *In Memoriam* contain few instances of interesting visually oriented passages. The prologue suggests the identity between Knowledge, Light, and God; and the epilogue relies on the convention of moonlight to illuminate a peaceful scene. Thus visual imagery introduces and concludes this sequence of linked lyrics, but the quality of these sections is such that one hesitates to claim much for either end of the frame.

Idylls of the King represents the culmination of Tennyson's life work, coming last in a line of long generic experiments and occupying his imagination for relatively longer than any other major poem. The role of word-paintings in this primarily narrative poem reveals the fate of this feature in his poetry. Their characteristic forms and functions in this work offer a summary of Tennyson's development of visually oriented description.

Word-paintings occupy an extremely important place in the general topography of *Idylls of the King* and indicate Tennyson's mastery of the form. They weave through the narrative, evolving toward more fusion with story (much like the movement we detected in Dickens's relationship between word-painting and narrative). It is not surprising that both major writers become more adept at bringing the narrative, lyric, and dramatic modes of literature together. But that each moves from reliance on picturesque word-paintings to word-portraits and then to symbolic uses of word-paintings presents a strikingly similar pattern.

Word-painting in *Idylls of the King* relates importantly to narrative, character development, theme, and form. In content it generally progresses from picturesque to visionary landscapes. In a neat correlation between content and form, Tennyson uses the older, picturesque, descriptive style to establish the early glory of Arthur's reign. Most of these long set pieces may be found in "Gareth and Lynette" in sections such as the cinematic views of Camelot, seen first in the distance, and then moving closer and closer with the hero. These descriptions contribute to the fairy-tale atmosphere of this early idyll, with its sense of endless time for leisurely descriptions akin to modes of courtly romance. Tennyson clearly enjoys spoofing the traditional sublime and the Gothic horror in his description of the Castle Perilous with which he concludes "Gareth and Lynette."

Whereas the early books of the idylls contain several such set pieces that function primarily to help us visualize an earlier time, later idylls, beginning with "Pelleas and Ettarre" speed up narrative, and word-painting becomes more truncated as the end of the Round Table approaches and vision becomes increasingly confused and doomful. Increasingly, Tennyson relies on word-portraits—frozen moments of dramatic climax, framed by doorway, window, or mirror—to underline turning points in the action or to crystallize a relationship. The relationship between Lancelot and Guinevere comes in most often for such treatment. Arthur, too, is shown in increasingly frozen attitudes as his ability to hold the Round Table together collapses, and he appears to lack the ability to act. Time and again we see Arthur and Guinevere enthroned (in early idylls), or Lancelot and Guinevere glimpsed obliquely through an oriel or framed in a garden scene reminiscent of the tableaux vivants we have described in Dickens's narratives. These scenes help the reader recognize and retain significant climaxes in an often-confusing story. At least in the case of Lancelot and Guinevere, one suspects that the frame helps distance the eroticism of the illicit relationship and partly neutralize its threat to the Round Table. The frame works only for a time.

The most complex use Tennyson makes of visually oriented descriptive materials, however, relates our feature most intimately to its ongoing narrative. Tennyson uses word-paintings in *Idylls of the King* to escape the temporal structure on which his story of Arthur is predicated. Most word-paintings, especially in the middle and late idylls, appear embedded in chaotic visions, ambiguous dreams, and flashbacks narrated by a character. Visions, dreams, and flashbacks serve to unite the sprawling narrative by recalling early prophesies (such as those concerning Arthur, for example), or foreshadowing the outcome of the last battle or the end of the Round Table. In addition, word-paintings, embedded either in flashbacks or in epic similes which structure many of these descriptions, dramatize the grimness of the present (see "The Last Tournament," for example) by contrasting it with the summer of Arthur's reign. Memories of the vivid sensuality of Guinevere's arrival at Camelot in May build nostalgia for an earlier, more innocent time. Thus, flashbacks aggrandize the past, contrast with the present, and anticipate an ever more dismal future.

Visionary or dream landscapes—another favorite matrix for word-paintings in *Idylls of the King*—also open vistas into another time.[22] Merlin, Leodogran, Enid, Pelleas, Tristram, Guinevere—all these characters have dreams that anticipate future action, action increasingly doomful as the idylls progress. "The Holy Grail," the only idyll whose very structure is visionary, tells its story through descriptions of five visions visited upon the nun, Galahad, Percivale, Lancelot, and Bors as they search for the Holy Grail. "The Holy Grail" concludes this section of my study because it anticipates Modernist verse.

Everywhere in *Idylls of the King*, word-painting helps link the segmented narrative through recurrent imagery. A study of word-painting in this work reveals that *Idylls* is no less elegaic than was *In Memoriam*. Whereas *In Memoriam* focuses on the movement from personal grief to compensation for loss, *Idylls* traces the defeat of idealism in an imperfect world, and offers at least a suggestion of contemporary vision that includes a whole culture. In both poems, extended visually oriented description mirrors the general progression of mood and theme by offering analogues to internal states of mind. Although this movement evolves from grief to hope in *In Memoriam* and from hope to highly qualified optimism in *Idylls*, Tennyson carefully correlates mood of landscape and patterns of imagery in both long works.

The generally fragmented, dark, wintry natural world of *In Memoriam* reflects the speaker's inability to see beyond his own grief for the first year after Hallam's death. A gradual introduction of springtime motifs indicates his parallel rebirth to the beauties of life around him. Recurrent imagery expresses the progress of a soul—or, in modern terms, a self—from grief, through the stages of mourning, to the rebirth of hope and faith in immortality. As we have seen, brief images in the structure of linked lyrics build our sense of this progress, but *In Memoriam* paints only a few extended word-paintings. These are strategically placed as catalysts for climactic moments of vision in the lyrical sequence.

In contrast, Tennyson relies rather heavily in *Idylls of the King* on all the different kinds of word-paintings I have identified in this study. Its structure weaves themes, paired characters, and recurrent imagery through twelve books, each given to a segment of the story of King Arthur. Whereas *In Memoriam* moves from winter to spring, the movement is just the reverse in *Idylls.* Tennyson himself explains the overall imagaic pattern he pursues: "The Coming of Arthur is on the night of the New Year; when he is wedded 'the world is white with May'; on a summer night the vision of the Holy Grail appears; and the 'Last Tournament' is in the 'yellowing autumn-tide.' Guinevere flees through the mists of autumn, and Arthur's death takes place at midnight in mid-winter" (Ricks, p. 1470). It is important to bear this general pattern of imagery in mind as we examine word-paintings in *Idylls,* but brief flashes of visual imagery will not concern us here. Several idylls ("Merlin and Vivien" and "The Last Tournament," for example) begin with extended visually oriented descriptions that set the mood and place for the idyll, a placement characteristic of some of Tennyson's earlier word-paintings ("Oenone," for example). In general, these extended landscape descriptions express the movement from the landscape of summer—optimism, light, and joy—to the darkening seasons that begin with "Balin and Balan" (significantly, the idyll written last)—increasingly pessimistic concerning the civilization Arthur and his Knights represent. Even the changing modes of description of battle or joust scenes echo the downward progress of the narrative and the imagery from clarity to obscurity.

The relationship between modes of word-painting and the theme of *Idylls* is clear. Throughout *Idylls,* Tennyson reiterates the deceptive nature of vision. Beginning with "The Coming of Arthur," characters constantly question the nature of reality and of truth.[23] Indeed, the frame idylls emphasize this theme of "right vision." Arthur dazes the sight of his followers, Leodogran "sees" the truth of Arthur's kingliness in a dream, and *Idylls* ends with that strangely ambiguous vision of Bedivere, who "saw . . . or *thought* he saw" (emphasis mine) Arthur merging into the sun that brings the New Year. Even Tennyson's comments to Victoria about *Idylls* emphasize the ambiguity at their visual center, saying, "the goal of this great world / lies beyond sight" ("To the Queen," pp. 1755–56).

Therefore, in the word-paintings of *Idylls of the King,* the quality of vision helps clarify the theme of the individual's search for a proper vision of society and God. "Guinevere" recapitulates the entire story, re-viewing those tales of the coming of Arthur with significant changes in their visual texture, as a sign that the bright word-paintings of the reign's youth have already been compromised by actions and by the distortions of memory. Interestingly, the story line compels us forward in *Idylls,* but it is the bright pictures of Arthur and Camelot that we may remember the longest. In this sense, *Idylls of the King* is elegaic—or perhaps merely nostalgic—for the certainties and beauties of a more innocent age.

The most interesting, most sophisticated, and most extensive relationship between word-painting and narrative occurs in "The Holy Grail." The three other idylls that include an extensive use of visually oriented materials—"The Coming of Arthur," "Merlin and Vivien," and "The Passing of Arthur"—use word-painting rather more simply. In "Merlin and Vivien," for example, nature itself is used expressionistically, both objectifying the heated emotions of the two main characters and forcing the denouement of the action. A brief look at sections of this idyll illustrates how Tennyson uses visual materials to emphasize the coherence of his narrative.

"Merlin and Vivien" opens with a description of setting for the dialogue between the two characters. An oncoming storm underlies their relationship.

> A storm was coming, but the winds were still,
> And in the wild woods of Broceliande,
> Before an oak, so hollow, huge and old
> It looked a tower of ivied masonwork,
> At Merlin's feet the wily Vivien lay.

(ll. 1–5)

The two hundred lines that follow this brief opening description constitute a flashback which relates how Vivien came to Camelot from the court of Mark to sow dissension. Two brief passages within this flashback illustrate Tennyson's use of word-paintings in *Idylls of the King* to foreshadow future actions, or to give us an image of significant moments in the past.

The first passage exemplifies the use of frozen verbal tableaux of Lancelot and Guinevere to frame action by architectural elements and simultaneously to distance scenes by the pastness of the narration.

> She past; and Vivien murmured after, 'Go!
> I bide the while.' Then through the portal-arch
> Peering askance, and muttering broken-wise,
> As one that labours with an evil dream,
> Beheld the Queen and Lancelot get to horse.

(ll. 96–100)

The recounting of Merlin's troubled dream, on the other hand, contains images that foreshadow the last battle.

> Then fell on Merlin a great melancholy;
> He walked with dreams and darkness, and he found
> A doom that ever poised itself to fall,
> An ever-moaning battle in the mist,
> World-war of dying flesh against the life,
> Death in all life and lying in all love,

The meanest having power upon the highest,
And the high purpose broken by the worm.

(ll. 187–94)

The visions in Merlin's dream reiterate the coming catastrophe in terms that eventually underscore the inevitability of that disaster. The last line of this passage presents another example of how subtly Tennyson uses visual imagery to recall details of the narrative. The "worm" to which Merlin refers connects with the striking passage later in "Guinevere," which re-views the whole story of the Round Table, including the dramatic moment when Lancelot plucks Modred from the top of the garden wall where he is spying on the Queen:

> . . . more than this
> He saw not, for Sir Lancelot passing by
> Spied where he couched, and as the gardener's hand
> Picks from the colewort a green caterpillar,
> So from the high wall and the flowering grove
> Of grasses Lancelot plucked him by the heel,
> And cast him as a worm upon the way;

(ll. 29–35)

It is the "wormlike" Modred, of course, who will serve as the immediate vehicle of the destruction of Arthur's order, although he is aided by the corruption that eats the Round Table from within, and by "the wily Vivien," who creeps through Camelot, sowing suspicion like the serpent whose imagery describes her.

The storm that eventually breaks at the end of "Merlin and Vivien" objectifies the storm within both characters and helps to determine Merlin's seduction by the evil temptress and by his own imperfect tendencies. "The Holy Grail," on the other hand, interests the student of word-painting because visionary materials determine both content and structure. In addition, this idyll appropriately concludes the present discussion of Tennyson because it is the most modern idyll in its imagery and in its manipulation of narrative in relation to the word-paintings it builds.

Visually oriented passages in "Merlin and Vivien" underlie the mood and denouement of this idyll, but they do not compose word-paintings as we have previously defined the feature. "The Holy Grail," on the other hand, offers word-paintings and other visual materials as visionary substructure for myth, to extend the significance of the story of Arthur through space and time, and relate it, by suggestion only, to the story of Christ. Tennyson thought the poem "one of the most imaginative of my poems" (Ricks, headnote, p. 1661). Recognizing the difficulty of arriving at the meaning of this section, Tennyson told his son, Hallam, that "the key is to be found in a careful reading of Sir Percivale's visions" (Ricks, headnote, p. 1661). These visions take the form of juxtaposed word-paintings that build a structure of panels.

Visions suffuse "The Holy Grail," as the poet attempts to enact "The Reality of the Unseen" (Ricks, headnote, p. 1661). The idyll tells its story in a boldly original manner, relying on fragments of stories told by Percivale (therefore, at second-hand) to the monk Ambrosius before Percivale dies. We hear the story from Ambrosius, obviously now at third-hand. Elaborate frames — of which the widest is the frame of the past tense of narration — distance the listener and the reader from the visions of the Grail themselves, thereby rendering them simultaneously more mysterious and more credible. The centers of the story are Percivale's recounting of the visions of five seers: the nun who first sees the Grail, Galahad, Percivale himself, Bors, and Lancelot. Each person sees "according to their sight," as Arthur wisely notes at the end of the idyll.

Percivale recounts each visionary experience in a manner that retains its enigmatic quality. The narrators lure the reader on (just as the knights are lured into chasing the Grail), and by breaking off one story to begin the next, may figuratively "madden" the reader as the nun "has driven men mad" with her visionary intensity at the beginning of the idyll. Percivale conveys detailed visual information that circles around the Grail itself, yet sometimes omits the object at the center. In this way, Tennyson succeeds in suspending incredulity while at the same time leaving the Grail vision itself shrouded in ambiguity.

Word-painting in this idyll serves not as catalyst for visionary experience as it did in *In Memoriam*, but represents the experience itself, grounded in an enigmatic narrative matrix. This technique represents a new degree of fusion for our feature. The nun's vision, for example, vividly animates the reader's first sight of the Grail in convincing magical terms. Silvery music precedes the vision — the auditory being the most characteristic accompaniment to a fully realized Tennysonian word-painting — and the description emphasizes the sensuous extremes of cold and warmth:

> O never harp nor horn,
> Nor aught we blow with breath, or touch with hand,
> Was like that music as it came; and then
> Streamed through my cell a cold and silver beam,
> And down the long beam stole the Holy Grail,
> Rose-red with beatings in it, as if alive,
> Till all the white walls of my cell were dyed
> With rosy colours leaping on the wall;
> And then the music faded, and the Grail
> Past, and the beam decayed, and from the walls
> The rosy quiverings died into the night.

(ll. 113–23)

The sensuous specificity of this word-painting grounds subsequent visions in a technique similar to the one Tennyson used many years earlier in "The Kraken," where specific sense images deflect the reader's attention from the indeterminate object at the center, and the suggestiveness transfers from specific image to the whole visual composition.

A second word-painting in "The Holy Grail" provides one of the most detailed descriptions of the mighty hall at Camelot:

> For all the sacred mount of Camelot,
> And all the dim rich city, roof by roof,
> Tower after tower, spire beyond spire,
> By grove, and garden-lawn, and rushing brook,
> Climbs to the mighty hall that Merlin built.
> And four great zones of sculpture, set betwixt
> With many a mystic symbol, gird the hall:
> And in the lowest beasts are slaying men,
> And in the second men are slaying beasts,
> And on the third are warriors, perfect men,
> And on the fourth are men with growing wings,
> And over all one statue in the mould
> Of Arthur, made by Merlin, with a crown,
> And peaked wings pointed to the Northern Star.
> And eastward fronts the statue, and the crown
> And both the wings are made of gold, and flame
> At sunrise till the people in far fields,
> Wasted so often by the heathen hordes,
> Behold it, crying "We have still a King."
>
> (ll. 227–45)

Putting this description beside the early descriptions of "The Palace of Art" demonstrates the greater coherence of Tennyson's late word-paintings and their increased integration with narrative. The comparison also indicates the emergence of a symbolic technique fused with particular visual elements. For the description of the hall at Camelot clearly expresses a kind of allegory of the stages of development of the human spirit from barbarity to ideality. This allegory perfectly expresses—in the descriptive mode—the progress of the story of Arthur to the point when the Round Table begins to break apart. The word-painting of Camelot ought, also, to connect in the reader's mind with other pictures of Camelot scattered through *Idylls of the King* in order to build a precise sense of its features as well as to contrast with its sad decay toward the end of Arthur's reign.

Tennyson tells us that Percivale's visions are the key to the poem's mystical meaning, but his visions are ambiguous and difficult to understand. They take the form of four brief word-paintings: one, a picturesque panorama of lawn, brook, and apple tree; the second, an innocent and welcoming woman sitting spinning in a doorway; the next, a strangely obscured monumental figure of gold and jewels; the last, a walled city at the top of a hill where crowds cheer Percivale's arrival. All merely visions, these turn to dust as Percivale embraces them. Fragments of symbolic narration are apparent in this section of "The Holy Grail," but the reader is left to incorporate them into an interpretation. Tennyson felt the need to help his reader here, commenting, "The gratification of sensual appetite brings Percivale no content. Nor does wifely love and the love of the family; nor does wealth, which is worshipt by labour; nor does glory; nor does Fame" (Ricks, footnote, p. 1673). Word-painting fuses with narrative in this passage to become the means by which Tennyson conveys the failure of Percivale's spiritual search at this point in the narrative.

The story of Galahad interrupts the account of Percivale's quest, when the purest of all the Knights suddenly appears at the holy hermitage where Percivale rests from his search. Galahad also tells his story in the form of a word-painting. His tale incorporates many elements of Tennyson's sublime landscapes from earlier poetry to capture the awesomeness of Percivale's vision of Galahad, which shows the chosen one as he moves through an inimical wasteland and across a series of bridges that miraculously spring up before him across "the great Sea," and flare into fire after he crosses. The event is clearly visionary, for concrete earthly elements merge with divine ones ("shoutings of all the sons of God") that are logically inexplicable.

> There rose a hill that none but man could climb,
> Scarred with a hundred wintry water-courses—
> Storm at the top, and when we gained it, storm
> Round us and death; for every moment glanced
> His silver arms and gloomed: so quick and thick
> The lightnings here and there to left and right
> Struck, till the dry old trunks about us, dead,
> Yea, rotten with a hundred years of death,
> Sprang into fire: and at the base we found
> On either hand, as far as eye could see,
> A great black swamp and of an evil smell,
> Part black, part whitened with the bones of men,
> Not to be crost, save that some ancient king
> Had built a way, where, linked with many a bridge,
> A thousand piers ran into the great Sea.
> And Galahad fled along them bridge by bridge,
> And every bridge as quickly as he crost
> Sprang into fire and vanished, though I yearned
> To follow; and thrice above him all the heavens
> Opened and blazed with thunder such as seemed
> Shoutings of all the sons of God . . .

(ll. 489–509)

The visual perspective of this passage is anchored by the point of view of Percivale, the one who is left behind to watch Galahad ascend into the heavens (much as Bedivere will watch Arthur sail into the sunrise at the end of *Idylls of the King*). Whereas Bedivere only thinks he sees the boat disappear into the sun, Percivale's purity and true-vision is finally rewarded with a vision of the Grail itself, hanging over Galahad.

and first
At once I saw him far on the great Sea,
In silver-shining armour starry-clear;
And o'er his head the Holy Vessel hung
Clothed in white samite or a luminous cloud.
And with exceeding swiftness ran the boat,
If boat it were—I saw not whence it came.
And when the heavens opened and blazed again
Roaring, I saw him like a silver star—
And had he set the sail, or had the boat
Become a living creature clad with wings?
And o'er his head the Holy Vessel hung
Redder than any rose, a joy to me,
For now I knew the veil had been withdrawn.

(ll. 509–22)

A vision of the Celestial City further rewards Percivale for his perseverence and concludes this section of the idyll.

Next Percivale recounts the vision of Sir Bors, but his narration lacks word-paintings. The two knights return to a half-ruined Camelot ("heaps of ruins, hornless unicorns, / cracked basilisks, and splintered cockatrices," etc.) and there they hear the last story of the search for the Grail. Each vision has added a climax to the idyll, but the vision of Sir Lancelot is the only one to rival the visionary intensity of Galahad's experience and Percivale's perception of it. Lancelot describes another wasteland to put beside Percivale's:

and then I came
All in my folly to the naked shore,
Wide flats, where nothing but coarse grasses grew;
But such a blast, my King, began to blow,
So loud a blast along the shore and sea,
Ye could not hear the waters for all the blast,
Though heapt in mounds and ridges all the sea
Drove like a cataract, and all the sand
Swept like a river, and the clouded heavens
Were shaken with the motion and the sound.

(ll. 789–98)

The scene is again the shore of a sea, returning us to that favorite Tennyson locale which has formed the basis for word-paintings from *The Devil and the Lady* right through *Idylls of the King*. A conveniently placed boat conveys Lancelot to Carbonek, legendary home of the Grail, an enchanted and abandoned place standing in moonlight:

Seven days I drove along the dreary deep,
And with me drove the moon and all the stars;
And the wind fell, and on the seventh night
I heard the shingle grinding in the surge,

> And felt the boat shock earth, and looking up,
> Behold, the enchanted towers of Carbonek,
> A castle like a rock upon a rock,
> With chasm-like portals open to the sea,
> And steps that met the breaker! there was none
> Stood near it but a lion on each side
> That kept the entry, and the moon was full.
>
> (ll. 805–15)

Several motifs from earlier word-paintings recur here, and the setting reminds the reader of other sites for tests throughout *Idylls,* from the comic Castle Perilous to the chancel and broken cross where Arthur will lie and where, also, "the moon is full." Lancelot climbs through the silent castle to the "topmost tower," following a sound like a lark "as in a dream." But, when he finally enters:

> and through a stormy glare, a heat
> As from a seventimes-heated furnace, I,
> Blasted and burnt, and blinded as I was,
> With such a fierceness that I swooned away—
> O, yet methought I saw the Holy Grail,
> All palled in crimson samite, and around
> Great angels, awful shapes, and wings and eyes.
> And but for all my madness and my sin,
> And then my swooning, I had sworn I saw
> That which I saw; but what I saw was veiled
> And covered; and this Quest was not for me.
>
> (ll. 839–49)

Because Lancelot's sin has blurred his vision of truth, he sees only the outlines of the Grail, again, "according to his sight."

This vision constitutes the last word-painting in "The Holy Grail," but it remains, appropriately, to Arthur to sum up the perspective of the true visionary. Although he has not gone in search of the Grail himself, he understands the nature of the quest better than any of his knights because he understands the proper role of a king:

> Who may not wander from the allotted field
> Before his work be done; but, being done,
> Let visions of the night or of the day
> Come as they will; and many a time they come,
> Until this earth he walks on seems not earth,
> This light that strikes his eyeball is not light,
> This air that smites his forehead is not air
> But vision—yea, his very hand and foot—
> In moments when he feels he cannot die,
> And knows himself no vision to himself,
> Nor the high God a vision, nor that One
> Who rose again: ye have seen what ye have seen.
>
> (ll. 904–15)

"The Holy Grail" demonstrates Tennyson's most advanced use of word-painting. In a series of symbolic landscapes, he uses these visually oriented descriptions to suggest ideality in an imperfect world. He makes them the visionary substructure to myth, in order to extend the significance of Arthur's story through time and space. "The Holy Grail" is strikingly "modern" in its manipulation of narrative and in the important contribution word-painting makes to this aspect of composition.

In general, word-painting in *Idylls of the King* serves as a technique to escape the temporal structure of narrative. However, it also contributes to that narrative by recalling the past, foreshadowing the future, and providing coherence for a segmented, complex story. It is suggestive to conclude this study of Tennyson's word-paintings and their relationship to narrative as we began it, with the enigmatic image of the seer standing on the shore of an immense water, enclosed and protected by the landscape behind him. Dwarfed by the immensity of a nature that ultimately remains opaque to vision, he nonetheless bravely attempts to see a coherent pattern in the distance. Percivale, Bedivere, and Arthur all strain to extract meaning from the blurred outlines of the phenomenological world. Of the three, Bedivere is the last rewarded, for he thinks he sees Arthur merging with the image of light in the final moments of *Idylls of the King,* tentatively suggestive of the existence of a cyclical pattern in nature and human history that will some day see his return: "And the new sun rose bringing the new year."

Conclusion: Toward the Blending of Genres

This study originated from a fascination with formal parallels between visually oriented poetic and fictional descriptions and techniques employed in the visual arts. This interest, combined with Lessing's famous suggestion that painting realizes static form whereas poetry embodies kinesis first led me to wonder if word-painting might represent one area that belies Lessing's formula. For, it seemed to me, visually oriented language in the late eighteenth century and in the nineteenth century relies on painterly devices to establish a narrator/viewer whose coherent perspective allows him to scan foreground and background; to note contrasts between light and dark, between volume and mass; and whose own limits of vision frame the vista. This "narrator of landscape" operates somewhat as a painter who composes a landscape within the bounds of a single canvas. And, as the viewer visually explores the scene before him, does he not engage in a kind of metaphoric journey through the natural world, noting and commenting on those features that strike him? Might this not be kinesis within stasis? And might it not blur Lessing's neat distinction?

Two related issues then occurred to me. The first was whether each important writer or artist composes his word-paintings in a way characteristic of his habits of mind and in a characteristic style. Each writer might be expected to construct a different kind of word-painting. What might be the features of the word-paintings of Ann Radcliffe? Of Charles Dickens? Of Thomson or Tennyson? And, further, might eighteenth-century novelists and poets be partial to a different sort of word-painting than nineteenth-century writers?

The second issue relates to the large and compelling question of generic form. An interest in eclectic forms both in poetry and fiction characterizes nineteenth-century literature in England—and in America, too, if one considers *Moby Dick*! Due, perhaps, to the new dominance of the novel form, poets from Wordsworth through Tennyson, Yeats, and Eliot sought to include narrative materials in the predominantly lyrical mode of poetry to which the balladic tradition has always contributed significantly. Contrarily, novelists from the

Brontës through Dickens, Hardy, Lawrence, and Woolf include visually oriented descriptions in their novels. What might the combination of ongoing temporal narration with the "stopped time" of description contribute to the changing forms of nineteenth-century fiction and poetry? And, lastly, does word-painting contribute to the blurring of the genres of poetry and fiction and the resulting "hybrid" forms that characterize Modernist literature?

Since the generic problem has proved too grand in scope for the present study, it must await subsequent examination. This discussion concludes, instead, with a chronological summary of the characteristics of those word-painters considered in the preceding chapters, their contributions to the history of nineteenth-century word-painting, and a brief look at directions suggested by one representative Modernist work by Eliot and one by Woolf.

Ann Radcliffe, I contend, was one of the first novelists to raise word-painting to the status of a primary descriptive motif. The alternation of the modes of narration and description constitutes her chief compositional strategy, and her descriptions usually take the form of static catalogues of elements in a landscape. Occasionally, however, descriptions in *The Mysteries of Udolpho* take on the movement and coherence of a fully realized word-painting, where the eye of the observer progresses in an orderly fashion from visual element to visual element and succeeds in dramatizing the landscape itself as a kind of visual journey. Radcliffe's true word-paintings, of which there are five in the novel, invariably concern sublime landscape. They often represent narrative climaxes as well, a use of word-painting also characteristic of the nineteenth-century word-painters Wordsworth, Dickens, and Tennyson.

The alternation of modes and the imperfect integration of the mood of landscape with the attitudes of the heroine who views that scene in Radcliffe's novels offer basic strategies with which to compare subsequent efforts to fuse word-painting with thematic and formal concerns. Radcliffe's attempts to dramatize description and to infuse it with passion, however, suggest an impulse toward subjective landscape description which flowered in the Romantic period.

Thomson serves as innovative word-painter in the poetic tradition, much as Radcliffe serves for fiction. *The Seasons,* published roughly seventy years before *The Mysteries of Udolpho,* offers poets a compendium of subjects and styles with which to describe landscape objectively rendered. Thomson, who is relatively uninterested in narrative, combines quasi-scientific observation of natural phenomena with the varying moods of his largely uncharacterized observer. Personification lends structure to his observations, a strategy adopted by Woolf in the fragmented word-painting of *The Waves.* Thomson's word-paintings are pictorial in effect and their alternation with meditations upon their meanings echoes Radcliffe's alternation of modes later in the century. Thomson is memorable for his ability to capture the precise effects of light and color on a variegated landscape and for the personifying imagination that organizes those observations.

Wordsworth, representing the Romantic poets in this study, marks the shift from a generalized recording of landscape pictures to self-conscious reactions to nature. In "Tintern Abbey" and *The Prelude* one notes with surprise the relative dearth of fully realized word-paintings in the work of this "nature" poet, for his imagery is only intermittently visual. Like Radcliffe and Scott, however, Wordsworth utilizes the melding of sense impressions characteristic of a complete nineteenth-century word-painting. Wordsworth, Dickens, and Tennyson often include auditory impressions as accompaniment to visual ones, and sometimes fuse with them the impressions of smell, taste, and touch as well.

In Wordsworth's poetry, the landscape prominently begins to illuminate the state of mind of the viewer. When art shifts from a mimetic or pragmatic to an expressive emphasis at the beginning of the Romantic period, the emotions of the viewer become equally important—or ultimately more important—than the accurate recording of observed phenomena. Thus, viewer and phenomenological world cooperate to produce poetry that registers "both what they half create, / And what perceive," Wordsworth's famous prescription for the reciprocal workings of the world and the imagination in "Tintern Abbey." An emphasis on the subjective reading of landscape—landscape as "objective correlative" in Eliot's phrase—surfaces during the Romantic period.

Thomson's underlying personification has been replaced in Wordsworth's "Tintern Abbey" and *The Prelude* by the narrative of the growth of the poetic imagination. In *The Prelude,* the two fully realized word-paintings simultaneously represent climactic moments of insight, and sublimity serves as catalyst to a moment of mystical vision. Wordsworth struggles with language, in these passages, to convey essentially nonverbal moments of transport, and word-painting converts from an objective to a subjective truth. Tennyson's climactic word-painting in *In Memoriam* will register a similar moment.

My study's central findings concern the two greatest Victorian word-painters, Dickens and Tennyson, whose word-paintings, surveyed chronologically, reveal strikingly similar developments. Both writers retain their interest in word-paintings throughout their long writing careers. Both move from simple uses of visually oriented descriptions to increasingly complex ones; and a three-step development in the reliance on different kinds of word-paintings meshes when one considers works of their apprenticeships, their middle periods, and their late periods.

Not surprisingly, both writers' early word-paintings depend heavily on their common inheritance from an eighteenth-century picturesque tradition. *Barnaby Rudge,* an early historical fiction by Dickens, employs primarily picturesque modes to scene-paint historical panoramas. Similarly, Tennyson's apprenticeship poetry relies upon the picturesque conventions of the landscape tradition on which he drew for his entire career. In contrast to Dickens, the iconography of Tennyson's word-paintings is strikingly consistent throughout the canon. He is fond of prospect visions, and often locates his observer on a cliff or shore overlooking the "mighty deep," where he can capitalize on contrasts between heights and depths, darkness and light, motion and stasis, enclosure and expansiveness, and silence and sound in order to lend a sense of pictorial clarity and high drama to the description.

Works from the middle periods of Dickens and Tennyson indicate increasing mastery of the relationship between descriptive, narrative, and dramatic materials that is not surprising. But it is interesting that both writers utilize fewer picturesque word-paintings and substitute for these an extensive use of the word-portrait and the dramatic verbal tableau in works of the 1840s. Tennyson's *English Idylls* and *The Princess*, and Dickens's *David Copperfield*— works considered "transitional" in this study—often employ a similar technique to freeze climactic moments of narration borrowed from conventions popular in the mid-Victorian theatre. Perhaps this reflects a shift in interest from landscape to characterization in both writers. The three works just mentioned similarly incorporate traditional picturesque perspectives on landscape description and move toward more vividly dramatic fusions between landscape and human emotion.

Whereas Dickens continues to work within the conventions of the novel, Tennyson, in the late 1840s, becomes increasingly interested in working on questions that might lead to new formal possibilities for poetry, the mode then losing first place to the novel in Victorian culture. In a series of poetic experiments starting with *The Princess*, and moving through *In Memoriam, Maud,* and *Idylls of the King*, Tennyson begins to emphasize the long narrative poem, and to work on methods to fuse narrative with his primarily lyrical and descriptive genius. Many of his poems after 1854 fall between the ready categories of lyric, dramatic, or narrative verse. The "mixed" generic quality of his poetry opens possibilities for those poets who follow him, and word-paintings participate in the evolution toward a more symbolically oriented form.

In mature works by both writers, extended descriptions operate as recurrent symbolic motifs that often anticipate or unite narrative developments. Though no longer really word-paintings, visually oriented imagery sequences represent the next step in the development of the descriptive mode. Dickens's *Little Dorrit*, for example, utilizes the dominant pictorial motif of light and dark in such a way that its gradual alteration in meaning ultimately undercuts the superficial optimism of the novel's conclusion. Similarly, *In Memoriam* and *Idylls of the King* use reiterated visually oriented description to signal important, though opposing, shifts in mood. *In Memoriam* traces "the way of the soul" from despair to faith, and the imagery of the sequence alters to suggest the healing connection between man and nature. In *Idylls of the King*, on the other hand, truncated descriptions of an increasingly wasted landscape suggest the catastrophic end of Arthur and the Round Table, an end only slightly modified by the final vision of Arthur sailing into the sunrise of the new year. The word-paintings in *Idylls of the King* interestingly sum up Tennyson's development of the feature throughout his poetry, from the sublime set pieces and picturesque landscapes of the early idylls, to the visual tableaux of Lancelot, Guinevere, and Arthur at the height of their powers, to the reiterated visions and dreams that become prophetic symbols to unite the sections of the story. Word-painting breaks down with the fall of Camelot. "Guinevere," recapitulating the idylls, contrasts present confused visions with past clarity and prepares for the descent into darkness of the last battle.

Since most historical surveys conclude by hinting at developments to come, this study of Victorian word-painting ends with a brief preview of the fate of our feature in the post-Victorian period. T. S. Eliot offers a convenient link between our history of nineteenth-century word-painting and the questions of genre that interested the Modernists. It is fast becoming a critical commonplace that Eliot owes a tremendous poetic debt to Tennyson. But back in 1936 when Eliot praised Tennyson's ear and condemned his story telling, this debt was masked by the Modernist's disdain for the Victorian. Asserting that Tennyson "could not tell a story at all," Eliot announces that his poems "are always descriptive and always picturesque; they are never really narrative."[1] Eliot overstated his point, in my opinion; certainly Tennyson would have considered this strong censure and contrary to his intentions. Eliot may have found Tennyson's poetry wanting, but this did not deter him from borrowing extensively from Tennyson for his own narrative strategy in *The Waste Land*. From *In Memoriam* Eliot might have learned how to employ a segmented structure of "linked lyrics" (Eliot's phrase) and how to use recurrent images that gradually achieve the status of symbol. Tennyson and the Romantics might also have taught him how to use external landscape elements to represent internal states of consciousness, for Eliot's famous formulation concerning the objective correlative is well illustrated by Tennyson's "Mariana," as I have shown. And, from *Idylls of the King*, Eliot may have observed a way to link the fragmented images and symbols of the modern world through the underpinnings of myth.

Eliot uses a mythical story and a heroic or prophetic figure to provide coherence to the suggested narration of *The Waste Land* in much the same way that Tennyson uses the story of Arthur and the prophesies of Merlin and others to unite the segments of the story of *Idylls of the King*. Eliot tells us not only that Tiresias provides "the link between all the personages" in the poem, but also that Tiresias's perspective provides "the substance of the poem" (l. 52).[2] How close this is in conception to the idea that Leodogran's dream in "The Coming of Arthur" provides the perspective necessary to understanding Arthur's entire reign, or that Percivale's visions hold the central meaning of "The Holy Grail"! In addition, the heroic figure of the Fisher King adds coherence to *The Waste Land* as he sits upon the shore wondering how to set his lands in order.

Like Tennyson also, Eliot uses description—through increasingly truncated in form—both to suggest symbolic states of being and to suggest narrative progression. He sometimes includes a frozen moment, an epiphany that transcends time, such as the famous moment in the Hyacinth garden:

> Yet when we came back, late, from the Hyacinth garden,
> Your arms full, and your hair wet, I could not
> Speak, and my eyes failed, I was neither
> Living nor dead, and I knew nothing,
> Looking into the heart of light, the silence.
>
> (WL, I, ll. 37–41)

The scene may remind us both of the center of "The Gardener's Daughter" and the moment on the lawn that precedes the climactic mystical vision in *In Memoriam.* Eliot's visionary moments are surely worthy to be set beside those of Wordsworth and Tennyson. Reiteration of the four elements—fire, water, earth, and air—gradually suggests a sense of the wholeness that lies behind the segmented structure of *The Waste Land.* Man, though estranged from Nature, at least may hope to purge his physical and spiritual thirst in the thunderstorm of the poem's conclusion, enigmatic though that storm may be.

Just as *The Waste Land* successfully blends narrative, descriptive, and lyrical elements in a single poem that expands the methods available to twentieth-century poets, so Virginia Woolf struggles against narrative in the novel tradition in order to achieve a hybrid form of writing she calls the "prosepoem." In a conscious effort to break out of the constraints of narrative form in the novel, Woolf deliberately subverts "story" in a preponderance of visually oriented description in her most experimental work, *The Waves.*[3] Six "consciousnesses" speak in turn in the nine "interchapters" that make up the body of the "prosepoem." These interchapters alternate with nine brief descriptive sections that Woolf designates "interludes." Woolf wrote these nine interludes as parts of a single word-painting, which she later divided in order to interlace them with the narratives of consciousness depicted in the interchapters.

As one can see from even this brief description of the forms of *The Waste Land* and *The Waves,* the relationship between description and narration remains a central issue for writers of both poetry and prose. Over a century after Ann Radcliffe wrote her novels, one finds Virginia Woolf solving the problem similarly: by the alternation between modes. Nine times in Woolf's prosepoem, she stops what little "story" there is in order to dwell on the look of a representative land- and seascape, whose terrain is described according to the metamorphosis of shape, color, and mass as light strikes it nine times in the single revolution of the sun from dawn to darkness. *The Waves* opens with the first interlude, beginning: "The sun had not yet risen. The sea was indistinguishable from the sky, except that the sea was slightly creased as if a cloth had wrinkles in it. Gradually as the sky whitened a dark line lay on the horizon dividing the sea from the sky and the grey cloth became barred with thick strokes moving, one after another, beneath the surface, following each other, pursuing each other" (p. 1). A kinetic narrative of landscape, this section of Woolf's word-painting demonstrates the enduring interest in visually oriented prose descriptions and brings us back full circle to Radcliffe's sublime land-scape visions to put beside Woolf's Impressionistic ones. But Ann Radcliffe and Virginia Woolf aim for widely divergent effects in their word-paintings and employ widely different strategies to compose them. Radcliffe's word-paintings rely on picturesque schemata and an eighteenth-century aesthetic of the sub-lime, whereas Woolf plays rather self-consciously with realistic, impressionis-tic, and expressionistic modes of vision transmitted from the painting theories of her day. Woolf's extended word-painting in *The Waves* constitutes a series of comments on the nature of perception itself.

In *The Waves* one derives narrative information primarily from the con-sciousness of Bernard, the would-be writer. But the reader is also privy to the minds of five other characters who sometimes speak in turn about the same events. This technique continues the structure of alternating fragments in the narrative as well as the descriptive mode. Although the six "consciousnesses" of *The Waves* never—with only one exception—speak directly to one another, each voice is distinguished by a characteristic set of visual motifs or themes. The interrelationships among these visual themes provide ultimate meaning for the work.

This description of the generation of meaning in *The Waves* is far closer to poetic technique than to the traditional narrative techniques of the nineteenth-century novel. Woolf gradually effects an interchange of significance between the interludes and the interchapters by constantly referring to the same visual motifs and symbols. The method eventually achieves a metaphoric unity impos-sible—and irrelevant—to Radcliffe's separate modes of description and narra-tion. This metaphoric unity is a Modernist strategy that arises partly from the innovative techniques for using word-paintings that I have demonstrated in the writings of Dickens and Tennyson. Word-painting contributes in this manner to the blurring of genres in works of some Modernist writers.

Woolf's assimilation of narrative and descriptive materials on a metaphoric level creates a static, nonnarrative effect when the narrative mode is subsumed by the descriptive. In describing this movement, one returns to Lessing's distinction with which this study began. The influence of word-paint-ing and the consequent fragmentation of narrative in works of Eliot and Woolf move both the novel and poetry toward a static form more characteristic of the visual arts—particularly of painting—than of the verbal arts of poetry and fic-tion (though the movement is more obvious in the case of fiction than in that of poetry).

The quality of the imagination exemplified by examining word-paintings by Radcliffe and Woolf and by Thomson and Eliot illustrates beautifully their differing conceptions of art. By implication the comparison also suggests the outline of the development of word-painting over two centuries. Radcliffe and Thomson represent the eighteenth-century aesthetic of balance and moderation, of the necessity of limiting the ecstasies and perils of the sublime by pairing them with the orderliness of the beautiful. Clarity of structure serves the god of self-control in Thomson, and presents the norm from which Radcliffe could "rebel" through passion. In contrast, Woolf and Eliot struggle to remain faithful to a more relativistic conception of human existence. Their view suggests that life is a ceaseless succession of sensations, that all is flux and duration. In order to experience life, according to this attitude, one must not create self-contained structures such as the structures of narrative art but, rather, one must attempt to register the fragmented truths of modern life, with its endless change. Woolf's formal solution was a simple and conservative descriptive mode of word-painting, interwoven with the restless and often cryptic impressions of consciousness. Eliot, on the other hand, chose a more boldly innovative path, a structure entirely constructed of fragments that expressed his vision of a modern hell where the individual is estranged from the natural world. Both Modernist writers use landscape as symbol for internal states of being, and both owe a debt to those writers who, going before them, each contributed some new possibility to a tradition of word-painting in English literature.

In the poetic as well as the fictional tradition, a concern with the proper balance between narration and description continues to evolve to the present day. Word-paintings help subvert narrative flow and move verbal art toward a more discontinuous, or "poetic," structure. One can no longer claim that narratives are the preserve of the novel or that description is a characteristic mode only of poetry. Writers continue to search restlessly for new forms that will integrate narration and description in provocative ways.

Notes

Works and organizations frequently cited have been identified by the following abbreviations:

BJRL	*Bulletin of the John Rylands University Library of Manchester*
ESC	*English Studies in Canada*
JAAC	*Journal of Aesthetics and Art Criticism*
JEGP	*Journal of English and German Philology*
MLA	Modern Language Association
MP	*Modern Poetry*
NCF	*Nineteenth-Century Fiction*
PBA	*Proceedings of the British Academy*
PL&L	*Papers on Language and Literature*
PMLA	*Publications of the Modern Language Association of America*
VP	*Victorian Poetry*
VS	*Victorian Studies*
WC	*The Wordsworth Circle*

Introduction

1. Erwin Panofsky, *Studies in Iconology* (New York: Oxford Univ. Press, 1939).

2. Gotthold Ephraim Lessing, *Laokoön,* ed. Dorothy Reich (Oxford: Oxford Univ. Press, 1965).

3. See Jean Hagstrum, *The Sister Arts* (Chicago: Univ. of Chicago Press, 1958) and Jeffrey B. Spencer, *Heroic Nature* (Evanston: Northwestern Univ. Press, 1973) for an outline of the tradition from Dryden to Gray and from Marvell to Thomson.

4. J. Hillis Miller, *The Form of Victorian Fiction* (Notre Dame: Univ. of Notre Dame Press, 1968); Barbara Hardy, *The Appropriate Form* (Evanston: Northwestern Univ. Press, 1971); George P. Landow, *Images of Crisis* (Boston: Routledge & Kegan Paul, 1982) and "There Began to Be a Great Talking about the Fine Arts," in *Mind and Art in Victorian England,* ed. Joseph L. Altholz (Minneapolis: Univ. of Minn. Press, 1976), 124–45; see also Landow, "Closing the Frame: Having Faith and Keeping Faith in Tennyson's 'The Passing of Arthur,'" *BJRL* 56 (1974), 423–42; F. E. L. Priestley, *Language and Structure in Tennyson's Poetry* (London: Andre Deutsch, 1973); Harold Bloom, *Poetry and Repression* (New Haven: Yale Univ. Press, 1976); W. David Shaw, *Tennyson's Style* (Ithaca: Cornell Univ. Press, 1976); Alan Sinfield, *The Language of Tennyson's* In Memoriam (Oxford: Oxford Univ. Press, 1971); Gerhard Joseph, "Victorian Frames: The Windows and Mirrors of Browning, Arnold, and Tennyson," *VP* 16 (1978), 70–80.

5. Emile Mâle, *The Gothic Image,* trans. Dora Nussey (New York: Harper & Row, 1958); Mario Praz, *The Romantic Agony* (Oxford: Oxford Univ. Press, 1951); Rensselaer W. Lee, "Ut Pictura Poesis: The Humanistic Theory of Painting," *Art Bulletin* XXII (1940), 197–269; Jean Hagstrum, *The Sister Arts.*

6. Joseph Frank, "Spatial Form in Modern Literature" in *The Widening Gyre* (Bloomington: Indiana Univ. Press, 1963), 3–63; Wylie Sypher, *Four Stages of Rennaissance Style* (New York: Doubleday, 1955); Boris Uspensky, *A Poetics of Composition,* trans. Valentina Zavarin and Susan Wittig (Berkeley: Univ. of Calif. Press, 1973); Meyer Schapiro, *Words and Pictures* (Paris: Mouton, 1973).

7. An increasing number of interart studies since 1980 suggests growing interest in this topic. See, for example, promising approaches by Marianna Torgovnick (*The Visual Arts, Pictorialism and the Novel: James, Lawrence and Woolf* [Princeton: Princeton Univ. Press, 1985]) and Wendy Steiner (*The Colors of Rhetoric: Problems in the Relation of Modern Literature and Painting* [Chicago: Univ. of Chicago Press, 1982]).

8. René Wellek and Austen Warren, *Theory of Literature* (New York: Harcourt Brace, 1956), 134.

Chapter 1

1. Unless otherwise stated, prose by Jane Austen is quoted from *Northanger Abbey* (New York: Dell, 1962); that of Ann Radcliffe from *The Mysteries of Udolpho: A Romance* (New York: Oxford Univ. Press, 1970); that of Walter Scott from *The Heart of Midlothian* (New York: Holt, Rinehart and Winston, 1965).

2. Alan Spiegel, *Fiction and the Camera Eye: Visual Consciousness in Film and the Modern Novel* (Charlottesville: Univ. of Virginia Press, 1976), 33.

3. Word-paintings are found on pp. 1–5, 175–76, 224–28, 263–70, and 596–604 of the authoritative Oxford edition.

4. Walter Scott, quoted by Bonamy Dobree, "Introduction," *The Mysteries of Udolpho* (New York: Oxford Univ. Press, 1970), x.

Chapter 2

1. Gordon Spence, "Introduction," Charles Dickens, *Barnaby Rudge* (Suffolk: The Chaucer Press, 1975), 14–15. Unless otherwise stated, the prose of Dickens is quoted from this standard edition, based on the "Charles Dickens Edition" of 1868, revised by the author.

2. See George Landow, *Images of Crisis* (Boston: Routledge and Kegan Paul, 1982) for references to Dickens and the cultural prevalence of such conventions.

3. Gordon Spence, "Introduction," *Barnaby Rudge* (Suffolk: The Chaucer Press, 1975), 18.

4. For a brief history of the development of this feature, see Jonathan E. Hill, "Cruikshank, Ainsworth, and Tableau Illustration," *VS* 23:4 (1980), 429–59.

5. Jerome Thale, "The Imagination of Charles Dickens: Some Preliminary Discriminations," *NCF* 15 (1967), 30–45.

6. For detailed discussion of this point, see John Butt and Kathleen Tillotson, *Dickens at Work* (London: Methuen, 1957) and Harvey Peter Sucksmith, *The Narrative Art of Charles Dickens* (Oxford: Oxford Univ. Press, 1970).

7. Charles Dickens, *David Copperfield* (New York: Houghton Mifflin, 1958). Unless otherwise stated, quotations from the novel will be taken from this edition, which is based on the standard text revised by Dickens for the edition of 1868–70.

8. Raymond Williams, in *The Country and the City* (New York: Oxford Univ. Press, 1973), points to these clusters of values as characteristic of the Dickens world view.

9. Michael Irwin, *Picturing: Description and Illusion in the Nineteenth-Century Novel* (London: Allen and Unwin, 1979), 105.

10. J. R. Harvey, *Victorian Novelists and Their Illustrators* (New York: N.Y. Univ. Press, 1971), 142–51.

11. Jerome Buckley, *The Victorian Temper* (Cambridge: Harvard Univ. Press, 1969), 29.

12. Harvey, 142. Harvey corroborates my formulation that the dramatic tableau underlies both H. K. Browne's illustrations for *David Copperfield* and the verbal visualizations of scenes.

13. J. Hillis Miller, *Charles Dickens: The World of His Novels* (Cambridge, Mass.: Harvard Univ. Press, 1958), 225.

14. Designated by Miller as central symbolic metaphors for *Little Dorrit*.

15. Charles Dickens, *Little Dorrit* (Suffolk: The Chaucer Press, 1967). Unless ortherwise stated, quotations from the novel will be taken from this edition, based on the "Charles Dickens Edition" of 1868.

16. Edmund Wilson, "Dickens: The Two Scrooges," in *The Wound and the Bow* (Cambridge, Mass.: Harvard Univ. Press, 1941), 30.

17. Mario Praz, *The Hero in Eclipse in Victorian Fiction* (London: Oxford Univ. Press, 1956), 58.

Chapter 3

1. H. M. McLuhan, "Tennyson and Picturesque Poetry," in *Critical Essays on the Poetry of Tennyson,* ed. John Killham (London: Routledge and Kegan Paul, 1960), 69.

2. Jean Hagstrum, *The Sister Arts* (Chicago: Univ. of Chicago Press, 1958); Ralph Cohen, *The Art of Discrimination* (London: Routledge & Kegan Paul, 1964); Marjorie Hope Nicholson, *Mountain Gloom and Mountain Glory* (Ithaca: Cornell Univ. Press, 1959); Jeffrey B. Spencer, *Heroic Nature* (Evanston: Northwestern Univ. Press, 1973).

3. Unless otherwise stated, the poetry of James Thomson is quoted from *The Complete Poetical Works,* ed. J. Logie Robertson (London: Oxford Univ. Press, 1951).

4. Unless otherwise stated, the poetry of William Wordsworth is quoted from *The Poetical Works of William Wordsworth,* ed. Ernest de Selincourt (Oxford: Clarendon Press, 1944).

5. Carlos Baker, "Sensation and Vision in Wordsworth," in *English Romantic Poets,* ed. M. H. Abrams (New York: Oxford Univ. Press, 1960), 107.

6. L. J. Swingle, "Wordsworth's 'Picture of the Mind,'" in *Images of Romanticism,* ed. Kroeber and Walling (New Haven: Yale Univ. Press, 1978), 87.

7. William Wordsworth, *The Prelude or Growth of a Poet's Mind,* ed. Ernest de Selincourt (Oxford: Clarendon Press, 1926). Subsequent references to *The Prelude* will be taken from this authoritative text, which prints the authorized text (1850) on the right-hand page and the text as read to Coleridge at Coleorton (1806–7) on the left-hand page.

8. Swingle, "Wordsworth's 'Picture of the Mind,'" 90.

9. Geoffrey H. Hartman, *Wordsworth's Poetry 1787–1814* (New Haven: Yale Univ. Press, 1964), 163.

Chapter 4

1. H. M. McLuhan, "Tennyson and Picturesque Poetry," in *Critical Essays on the Poetry of Tennyson,* ed. John Killham (London: Routledge & Kegan Paul, 1960), 67–86.

2. Unless otherwise stated, the poetry of Alfred, Lord Tennyson is quoted from *The Poems of Tennyson,* ed. Christopher Ricks (New York: Norton, 1969). All subsequent references to Tennyson's poetry will be taken from this, the authoritative modern text.

3. Ricks, *Tennyson,* 59n.

4. Ricks remarks that Tennyson includes a note on Ossian and Ann Radcliffe, "which may not be quoted," (T. Ms.) but which might reveal how Tennyson viewed the writings of Radcliffe.

5. A. Dwight Culler, *The Poetry of Tennyson* (New Haven: Yale Univ. Press, 1977), 42.

6. Harold Bloom, *Poetry and Repression* (New Haven: Yale Univ. Press, 1976), 42.

7. Carol Christ, *The Finer Optic* (New Haven: Yale Univ. Press, 1975), 12.

8. John D. Rosenberg, "Tennyson and the Landscape of Consciousness," *VP* 12 (1974), 303.

9. Valerie Pitt, *Tennyson Laureate* (London: Barrie & Rockliff, 1962), 22–26.

10. W. D. Paden, "Tennyson in Egypt: A Study of the Imagery in His Earlier Work," *Humanistic Studies* (1942), 71.

11. James D. Welch, "Tennyson's Landscapes of Time, and a Reading of 'The Kraken,'" *VP* 14:3 (1976), 198.

12. Douglas Bush, *Major British Writers* (London: Methuen, 1959), II, 380, cited by Ricks, 246.

13. Arthur Henry Hallam, *The Writings of Arthur Hallam,* ed. T. H. Vail Motter (New York: MLA, 1943), 87–139.

14. Edgar F. Shannon, Jr., "Poetry as Vision: Sight and Insight in 'The Lady of Shallot,'" *VP* 19 (1981), 223.

15. Is it mere coincidence that the colors of this poem are remarkably close to the primary colors of Rossetti's *Ecce Ancilla Domini?* Certainly we know that the Pre-Raphaelites loved Tennyson's "aesthetic" poems, and that the best illustration of this poem is Hunt's.

16. Robert Langbaum, *The Poetry of Experience* (New York: W. W. Norton & Co., 1957), 89–90.

17. I am indebted to Professor Juliet McMaster for pointing out that Tennyson suggests not only the languid movements of the Lotos-Eaters but the eye movements of the viewer who can make the waterfall "stop" by following its fall with her eyes.

18. F. E. L. Priestley, *Language and Structure in Tennyson's Poetry* (London: Andre Deutsch, 1973), 68.

19. Robert Bernard Martin, *Tennyson: The Unquiet Heart* (New York: Oxford Univ. Press, 1980), 189.

20. A. C. Bradley, "The Structure of *In Memoriam*," reprinted in *In Memoriam: An Authoritative Text, Backgrounds and Sources,* ed. Robert H. Ross (New York: W. W. Norton & Co., 1973), 193–200. Bradley suggests that we divide the lyrics into four groups as follows: #1–27: to the first Christmas—despair over death—emotional, subjective; #28–77: to the second Christmas—philosophical doubt—intellectual, objective; #78–103: to the third Christmas—nascent hope—emotional, subjective; #104–31: from the third Christmas—confident assertion of faith—intellectual, objective.

21. E. D. H. Johnson, "*In Memoriam:* The Way of the Poet," *VS* 2 (1958), 123.

22. W. David Shaw, *Tennyson's Style* (Ithaca: Cornell Univ. Press, 1976), 282; Gerhard Joseph, "Victorian Frames: The Windows and Mirrors of Browning, Arnold, and Tennyson," *VP* 16 (1978), 70–80.

23. George P. Landow, "Closing the Frame: Having Faith and Keeping Faith in Tennyson's 'The Passing of Arthur,'" *BJRL* 56 (1974), 423–42; John D. Rosenberg, *The Fall of Camelot* (Cambridge, Mass.: Harvard Univ. Press, 1973).

Conclusion

1. T. S. Eliot, *In Memoriam,* in *Selected Essays* (New York: Harcourt, Brace, 1950), 288.

2. Unless otherwise stated, the prose and poetry of T. S. Eliot is quoted from *The Complete Poems and Plays 1909–1950* (New York: Harcourt, Brace, 1952).

3. Unless otherwise stated, the prosepoetry of Virginia Woolf is quoted from *The Waves* (New York: Harcourt, Brace, 1923).

Bibliography

Abrams, M. H. *The Mirror and the Lamp: Romantic Theory and the Critical Tradition.* New York: Oxford Univ. Press, 1953.

————. *Natural Supernaturalism: Tradition and Revolution in Romantic Literature.* New York: Norton, 1971.

————, ed. *English Romantic Poets: Modern Essays in Criticism.* New York: Oxford Univ. Press, 1960.

Altholz, Joseph L., ed. *Mind and Art in Victorian England.* Minneapolis: Univ. of Minn. Press, 1976.

Arnheim, Rudolf. *Art and Visual Perception: A Psychology of the Creative Eye.* Berkeley: Univ. of Calif. Press, 1954.

————. *Visual Thinking.* Berkeley: Univ. of Calif. Press, 1969.

Auerbach, Erich. *Mimesis: The Representation of Reality in Western Literature.* Trans. by Willard R. Trask. Princeton: Princeton Univ. Press, 1953.

Austen, Jane. *Northanger Abbey.* 1803. New York: Dell, 1962.

Beach, Joseph Warren. *The Concept of Nature in Nineteenth-Century English Poetry.* New York: Pageant Books, 1936.

Bender, John B. *Spenser and Literary Pictorialism.* Princeton: Princeton Univ. Press, 1972.

Bloom, Harold. *Poetry and Repression.* New Haven: Yale Univ. Press, 1976.

————. *The Ringers in the Tower: Studies in the Romantic Tradition.* Chicago: Univ. of Chicago Press, 1971.

————, ed. *Romanticism and Consciousness: Essays in Criticism.* New York: Norton, 1970.

Booth, Wayne C. *The Rhetoric of Fiction.* Chicago: Univ. of Chicago Press, 1961.

Bradley, A. C. "The Structure of 'In Memoriam.'" *In Memoriam: An Authoritative Text, with Backgrounds and Sources.* Ed. Robert H. Ross. New York: Norton, 1973: 193–200.

Buckley, Jerome H. *Tennyson: The Growth of a Poet.* Cambridge: Harvard Univ. Press, 1960.

————. *The Triumph of Time: A Study of the Victorian Concepts of Time, History, Progress, and Decadence.* Cambridge: Harvard Univ. Press, 1966.

————. *The Victorian Temper.* Cambridge: Harvard Univ. Press, 1951.

————, ed. *The Worlds of Victorian Fiction.* Cambridge: Harvard Univ. Press, 1975.

Burke, Edmund. *A Philosophical Inquiry into the Origin of Our Ideas of the Sublime and the Beautiful.* Ed. J. T. Boulton. London: Routledge & Kegan Paul, 1958.

Bush, Douglas. *Major British Writers.* London: Methuen, 1959.

————. *Mythology and the Renaissance Tradition in English Poetry.* New York: Norton, 1932.

————. *Mythology and the Romantic Tradition in English Poetry.* New York: Norton, 1937.

Butt, John and Kathleen Tillotson. *Dickens at Work.* London: Methuen, 1957.

Carey, John. *Here Comes Dickens: The Imagination of a Novelist.* New York: Schocken, 1974.

Cary, Joyce. *Art and Reality: Ways of the Creative Process.* Garden City: Doubleday, 1958.

Caws, Mary Ann. *The Eye in the Text: Essays on Perception, Mannerist to Modern.* Princeton: Princeton Univ. Press, 1981.

Chatman, Seymour, ed. *Literary Style: A Symposium.* Oxford: Oxford Univ. Press, 1971.

Christ, Carol T. *The Finer Optic: The Aesthetic of Particularity in Victorian Poetry.* New Haven: Yale Univ. Press, 1975.

Clark, Kenneth. *Landscape into Art.* Boston: Beacon Press, 1949.

Cohen, Ralph. *The Art of Discrimination: Thomson's "The Seasons" and the Language of Criticism.* London: Routledge & Kegan Paul, 1964.

Collins, Philip. *Dickens: The Critical Heritage.* New York: Barnes & Noble, 1971.

Culler, A. Dwight. *The Poetry of Tennyson.* New Haven: Yale Univ. Press, 1977.

Davis, Robert Con. "The Structure of the Picturesque: Dorothy Wordsworth's Journals." *WC* IX: 1 (1978): 45–50.

Dawson, Carl. *Victorian Noon: English Literature in 1850.* Baltimore: Johns Hopkins Univ. Press, 1979.

Deane, C. V., ed. *Aspects of Eighteenth-Century Nature Poetry.* New York: Barnes & Noble, 1935.

deLaura, David, ed. *Victorian Prose: A Guide to Research.* New York: MLA, 1973.

Dickens, Charles. *Barnaby Rudge.* Suffolk: The Chaucer Press, 1975.

———. *David Copperfield.* New York: Houghton Mifflin, 1958.

———. *Little Dorrit.* Suffolk: The Chaucer Press, 1967.

Dyson, A. E. *Dickens: Modern Judgements.* London: Macmillan, 1968.

Eliot, Thomas Stearns. *The Complete Poems and Plays 1909–1950.* New York: Harcourt Brace, 1952.

———. *Selected Essays.* New York: Harcourt Brace, 1950.

Erdman, David. *A Bibliography of the Relations of Literature and the Other Arts.* New York: MLA, 1959.

Faverty, Frederic E. *The Victorian Poets: A Guide to Research.* Second Edition. Cambridge: Harvard Univ. Press, 1969.

Findlay, L. M. "Aspects of Analogy: The Changing Role of the Sister Arts Tradition in Victorian Criticism." *ESC* 3 (1976): 51–68.

Foakes, R. A. "The Power of Prospect: Wordsworth's Visionary Poetry." *The Author in His Work: Essays on a Problem in Criticism.* Ed. Louis L. Martz and Aubrey Williams. New Haven: Yale Univ. Press, 1978: 123–41.

Forster, John. *The Life of Charles Dickens.* London: Dent, 1927.

Frank, Joseph. "Spatial Form in Modern Literature." *The Widening Gyre.* Bloomington: Indiana Univ. Press, 1963: 3–63.

Fredeman, William E. *Pre-Raphaelitism: A Bibliocritical Study.* Cambridge: Harvard Univ. Press, 1965.

Freedman, Ralph. *The Lyrical Novel: Studies in Hermann Hesse, André Gide and Virginia Woolf.* Princeton: Princeton Univ. Press, 1963.

Freeman, Rosemary. *English Emblem Books.* London: Chatto & Windus, 1948.

Fry, Roger. *Transformations: Critical and Speculative Essays on Art.* London: Chatto & Windus, 1926.

———. *Vision and Design.* New York: Chatto & Windus, 1920.

Frye, Northrop. *Anatomy of Criticism: Four Essays.* Princeton: Princeton Univ. Press, 1957.

Frye, Roland Mushat. *Milton's Imagery and the Visual Arts: Iconographic Tradition in the Epic Poems.* Princeton: Princeton Univ. Press, 1978.

Gombrich, E. H. *Art and Illusion.* Princeton: Princeton Univ. Press, 1959.

Goslee, David F. "Spatial and Temporal Vision in Early Tennyson." *VP* 11 (1973): 323–29.

Hagstrum, Jean. *The Sister Arts: The Tradition of Literary Pictorialism and English Poetry from Dryden to Gray.* Chicago: Univ. of Chicago Press, 1958.

Hallam, Arthur. *The Writings of Arthur Hallam*. Ed. T. H. Vail Motter. New York: MLA, 1943.

Hardy, Barbara. *The Appropriate Form*. Evanston: Northwestern Univ. Press, 1971.

———. *Tellers and Listeners: The Narrative Imagination*. London: Univ. of London Press, 1975.

Hargrove, Nancy Duvall. *Landscape as Symbol in the Poetry of T. S. Eliot*. Jackson: Univ. Press of Mississippi, 1978.

Hartman, Geoffrey H. *The Unmediated Vision: An Interpretation of Wordsworth, Hopkins, Rilke & Valery*. New Haven: Yale Univ. Press, 1954.

———. *Wordsworth's Poetry 1787–1814*. New Haven: Yale Univ. Press, 1964.

Harvey, John. *Victorian Novelists and Their Illustrators*. New York: N.Y. Univ. Press, 1971.

Henkle, Roger B. *Comedy and Culture: England 1820–1900*. Princeton: Princeton Univ. Press, 1980.

Herring, Paul D. "Dickens' Monthly Number Plans for *Little Dorrit*." *MP* 64 (1966): 22–63.

Hill, Jonathan. "Cruikshank, Ainsworth, and Tableau Illustration." *VS* 23:4 (1980): 429–61.

Hipple, Walter John, Jr. *The Beautiful, the Sublime, and the Picturesque in Eighteenth-Century British Aesthetic Theory*. Carbondale: So. Illinois Univ. Press, 1957.

Holloway, John. *The Victorian Sage: Studies in Argument*. London: Macmillan, 1953.

Houghton, Walter E. *The Victorian Frame of Mind*. New Haven: Yale Univ. Press, 1963.

House, Humphrey. *The Dickens World*. London: Oxford Univ. Press, 1942.

Hunt, John Dixon. *The Figure in the Landscape: Poetry, Painting, and Gardening during the Eighteenth Century*. Baltimore: Johns Hopkins Univ. Press, 1976.

———, ed. *Encounters: Essays on Literature and the Visual Arts*. New York: Norton, 1971.

Hussey, Christopher. *The Picturesque: Studies in a Point of View*. New York: Putnam's Sons, 1927.

Irwin, Michael. *Picturing: Description and Illusion in the Nineteenth-Century Novel*. London: Allen & Unwin, 1979.

Johnson, E. D. H. "Alfred, Lord Tennyson." *The Victorian Poets: A Guide to Research*. Ed. Frederick E. Faverty. Second Edition. Cambridge: Harvard Univ. Press, 1968.

———. *The Alien Vision of Victorian Poetry*. Princeton: Princeton Univ. Press, 1952.

———. "'In Memoriam': The Way of a Poet." *VS* 2 (1958): 120–53.

Johnson, Edgar. *Charles Dickens: His Tragedy and Triumph*. New York: Viking, 1977.

Jordan, Frank, ed. *The English Romantic Poets: A Review of Research and Criticism*. New York: MLA, 1972.

Joseph, Gerhard. *Tennysonian Love: The Strange Diagonal*. Minneapolis: Univ. of Minnesota Press, 1969.

———. "Tennyson's Optics: The Eagle's Gaze." *PMLA* 92 (1976): 420–28.

———. "Victorian Frames: The Windows and Mirrors of Browning, Arnold, and Tennyson." *VP* 16 (1978): 70–88.

Jump, John D., ed. *Tennyson: The Critical Heritage*. London: Routledge & Kegan Paul, 1967.

Kayser, Wolfgang. *The Grotesque in Art and Literature*. Bloomington: Indiana Univ. Press, 1963.

Kermode, Frank. *The Classic: Literary Images of Permanence and Change*. New York: Viking, 1975.

———. *Romantic Image*. London: Routledge & Kegan Paul, 1957.

———. *The Sense of an Ending: Studies in the Theory of Fiction*. New York: Oxford Univ. Press, 1967.

Kiely, Robert. *The Romantic Novel in England*. Cambridge: Harvard Univ. Press, 1972.

Killham, John. *Critical Essays on the Poetry of Tennyson*. London: Routledge & Kegan Paul, 1960.

———. *Tennyson and "The Princess": Reflections of an Age*. London: Univ. of London, Athlone Press, 1958.

Kincaid, James R. "Antithetical Criticism, Harold Bloom, and Victorian Poetry." *VP* 14:4 (1976): 365–82.

————. *Dickens and the Rhetoric of Laughter.* Oxford: Oxford Univ. Press, 1971.

Knoepflmacher, U. C. and G. B. Tennyson, eds. *Nature and the Victorian Imagination.* Berkeley: Univ. of Calif. Press, 1977.

Kroeber, Karl. *Romantic Landscape Vision.* Madison: Univ. of Wisconsin Press, 1975.

————. and William Walling. *Images of Romanticism.* New Haven: Yale Univ. Press, 1978.

Landow, George P. *The Aesthetic and Critical Theories of John Ruskin.* Princeton: Princeton Univ. Press, 1971.

————. "Closing the Frame: Having Faith and Keeping Faith in Tennyson's 'The Passing of Arthur.'" *BJRL* 56 (1974): 423–42.

————. *Images of Crisis: Literary Iconology, 1750 to the Present.* Boston: Routledge & Kegan Paul, 1982.

————. *Victorian Types, Victorian Shadows: Biblical Typology in Victorian Literature, Art and Thought.* Boston: Routledge & Kegan Paul, 1980.

Langbaum, Robert. *The Poetry of Experience.* New York: Norton, 1957.

Lee, Rensselaer W. "Ut Pictura Poesis: The Humanistic Theory of Painting." *Art Bulletin* 22 (1940): 197–269.

Lessing, Gotthold Ephraim. *Laokoön.* Ed. Dorothy Reich. Oxford: Oxford Univ. Press, 1965.

Levine, George and William Madden, eds. *The Art of Victorian Prose.* London: Oxford Univ. Press, 1968.

Lewalski, Barbara Kiefer. *Donne's "Anniversaries" and the Poetry of Praise: The Creation of a Symbolic Mode.* Princeton: Princeton Univ. Press, 1973.

————. *Milton's Brief Epic: The Genre, Meaning and Art of "Paradise Regained."* Providence: Brown Univ. Press, 1966.

Lodge, David. *Language of Fiction: Essays in Critical and Verbal Analysis of the English Novel.* New York: Columbia Univ. Press, 1966.

Lubbock, Percy. *The Craft of Fiction.* New York: Viking, 1921.

Mâle, Emile. *The Gothic Image.* Trans. Dora Nussey. New York: Harper & Row, 1958.

Manwaring, Elizabeth Wheeler. *Italian Landscape in Eighteenth-Century England: A Study Chiefly of the Influence of Claude Lorrain & Salvator Rosa on English Taste, 1700–1800.* New York: Oxford Univ. Press, 1925.

Marcus, Steven. *Dickens: From Pickwick to Dombey.* New York: Basic Books, 1965.

Martin, Robert Bernard. *Tennyson: The Unquiet Heart.* New York: Oxford Univ. Press, 1980.

McIntyre, Clara F. *Ann Radcliffe in Relation to Her Time.* New Haven: Yale Univ. Press, 1920.

McSweeney, Kerry. "The State of Tennyson Criticism." *PL&L* 10 (1974): 433–46.

Meisel, Martin. "Dickens' Roman Daughter." In *Realizations: Narrative, Pictorial, and Theatrical Arts in Nineteenth-Century England.* Princeton: Princeton Univ. Press, 1983: 302–22.

Meyers, Jeffrey. *Painting and the Novel.* New York: Harper & Row, 1975.

Miller, J. Hillis. *Charles Dickens: The World of His Novels.* Cambridge: Harvard Univ. Press, 1958.

————. *The Disappearance of God: Five Nineteenth Century Writers.* Cambridge: Harvard Univ. Press, 1963.

————. *The Form of Victorian Fiction.* Notre Dame: Univ. of Notre Dame Press, 1968.

———— and David Borowitz. *Charles Dickens and George Cruikshank.* Berkeley: Univ. of Calif. Press, 1971.

Murray, E. B. *Ann Radcliffe.* New York: Twayne, 1972.

Nicholson, Marjorie Hope. *Mountain Gloom and Mountain Glory: The Development of the Aesthetics of the Infinite.* Ithaca: Cornell Univ. Press, 1959.

Noyes, Russell. *Wordsworth and the Art of Landscape.* Bloomington: Indiana Univ. Press, 1968.

Ogden, Henry V. S. and Margaret S. Ogden. *English Taste in Landscape in the Seventeenth Century.* Ann Arbor: Univ. of Michigan Press, 1955.

Osborne, Harold. *Theory of Beauty: An Introduction to Aesthetics.* London: Routledge & Kegan Paul, 1952.

Owen, W. J. B. "Wordsworth's Aesthetics of Landscape." *WC* 7 (1976): 70–82.

Paden, W. D. "Tennyson in Egypt: A Study of the Imagery in His Earlier Work." *Humanistic Studies* 27 (1942).

Panofsky, Erwin. *Studies in Iconology: Humanistic Themes in the Art of the Renaissance.* New York: Oxford Univ. Press, 1939.

Park, Roy. "'Ut Pictura Poesis': The Nineteenth-Century Aftermath." *JAAC* 28 (1969): 155–64.

Partlow, Robert B. *Dickens, the Craftsman: Strategies of Presentation.* Carbondale: So. Illinois Univ. Press, 1970.

Pattison, Robert. *Tennyson and Tradition.* Cambridge: Harvard Univ. Press, 1979.

Paulson, Ronald. *Emblem and Expression: Meaning in English Art of the Eighteenth Century.* London: Thames & Hudson, 1975.

Peckham, Morse. *Man's Rage for Chaos.* New York: Schocken, 1967.

Perkins, David and Barbara Leondar, eds. *The Arts and Cognition.* Baltimore: Johns Hopkins Univ., 1977.

Pfordresher, John. *A Variorum Edition of Tennyson's* Idylls of the King. New York: Columbia Univ. Press, 1973.

Pitt, Valerie. *Tennyson Laureate.* London: Barrie & Rockliff, 1962.

Praz, Mario. *The Hero in Eclipse in Victorian Fiction.* London: Oxford Univ. Press, 1956.

———. *Mnemosyne: The Parallel between Literature and the Visual Arts.* Princeton: Princeton Univ. Press, 1970.

Price, Martin. "The Picturesque Moment." *From Sensibility to Romanticism.* Ed. Frederick W. Hilles and Harold Bloom. New York: Oxford Univ. Press, 1965: 254–92.

———, ed. *Dickens: A Collection of Critical Essays.* Englewood Cliffs: Prentice Hall, 1967.

Priestley, F. E. L. *Language and Structure in Tennyson's Poetry.* London: Andre Deutsch, 1973.

Radcliffe, Ann. *The Mysteries of Udolpho.* Ed. Bonamy Dobree. New York: Oxford Univ. Press, 1970.

Richmond, H. M. *Renaissance Landscapes: English Lyrics in a European Tradition.* Paris: Mouton, 1973.

Ricks, Christopher. *Tennyson.* New York: Norton, 1972.

———. "Tennyson's Methods of Composition." *PBA* 52 (1966): 209–30.

Robbe-Grillet, Alain. *For a New Novel: Essays on Fiction.* Trans. Richard Howard. New York: Grove Press, 1965.

Robinson, Forrest G. *The Shape of Things Known: Sidney's Apology in Its Philosophical Tradition.* Cambridge: Harvard Univ. Press, 1972.

Rosenberg, John D. *The Fall of Camelot.* Cambridge: Harvard Univ. Press, 1973.

———. "Tennyson and the Landscape of Consciousness." *VP* 12 (1974): 303–20.

———. "The Two Kingdoms of 'In Memoriam.'" *JEGP* 58 (1959): 228–40.

Ruskin, John. *The Art Criticism of John Ruskin.* Ed. Robert L. Herbert. Gloucester: Peter Smith, 1969.

———. *The Literary Criticism of John Ruskin.* Ed. Harold Bloom. New York: Norton, 1965.

———. *Modern Painters.* London: Dent, 1873. Vols. I & V.

Salvesen, Christopher. *The Landscape of Memory: A Study of Wordsworth's Poetry.* London: E. Arnold, 1965.

Schapiro, Meyer. *Words and Pictures: On the Literal and the Symbolic in the Illustration of a Text.* Paris: Mouton, 1973.

Scholes, Robert and Robert Kellogg. *The Nature of Narrative.* New York: Oxford Univ. Press, 1966.

Scott, Sir Walter. *The Heart of Midlothian.* 1818. New York: Holt, Rinehart and Winston, 1965.

Shannon, Edgar F., Jr. "Poetry as Vision: Sight and Insight in 'The Lady of Shalott.'" *VP* 19 (1981): 207–25.

Shaw, W. David. *Tennyson's Style.* Ithaca: Cornell Univ. Press, 1976.

Sinfield, Alan. *The Language of Tennyson's "In Memoriam."* Oxford: Oxford Univ. Press, 1971.

Smitten, Jeffrey R., and Ann Daghistany, eds. *Spatial Form in Narrative*. Ithaca: Cornell Univ. Press, 1981.

Spacks, Patricia Meyer. *The Insistence of Horror: Aspects of the Supernatural in Eighteenth-Century Poetry*. Cambridge: Harvard Univ. Press, 1963.

Spencer, Jeffrey B. *Heroic Nature: Ideal Landscape in English Poetry from Marvell to Thomson*. Evanston: Northwestern Univ. Press, 1973.

Spiegel, Alan. *Fiction and the Camera Eye: Visual Consciousness in Film and the Modern Novel*. Charlottesville: Univ. of Virginia Press, 1976.

Stein, Richard L. *The Ritual of Interpretation: The Fine Arts as Literature in Ruskin, Dante Gabriel Rossetti, and Pater*. Cambridge: Harvard Univ. Press, 1975.

Steiner, Wendy. *The Colors of Rhetoric: Problems in the Relation of Modern Literature and Painting*. Chicago: Univ. of Chicago Press: 1982.

Stevenson, Lionel, ed. *Victorian Fiction: A Guide to Research*. Cambridge: Harvard Univ. Press, 1964.

Stewart, Garrett. *Charles Dickens and the Trials of the Imagination*. Cambridge: Harvard Univ. Press, 1974.

Stoehr, Taylor. *Dickens: The Dreamer's Stance*. Ithaca: Cornell Univ. Press, 1965.

Sucksmith, Harvey Peter. *The Narrative Art of Charles Dickens: The Rhetoric of Sympathy and Irony in His Novels*. Oxford: Oxford Univ. Press, 1970.

Sutton, Walter. "The Literary Image and the Reader: A Consideration of the Theory of Spatial Form." *JAAC* 16 (1957–58): 112–23.

Sypher, Wylie. *Four Stages of Renaissance Style*. Garden City: Doubleday, 1955.

Tennyson, Alfred Lord. *The Poems of Tennyson*. Ed. Christopher Ricks. New York: Norton, 1969.

Tennyson, Charles. *Alfred Tennyson*. New York: Macmillan, 1949.

———— and Christine Fall. *Alfred Tennyson: An Annotated Bibliography*. Athens: Univ. of Georgia Press, 1967.

Tennyson, Hallam, Lord. *Alfred Lord Tennyson: A Memoir by His Son*. London: Macmillan, 1897 and 1905.

Thale, Jerome. "The Imagination of Charles Dickens: Some Preliminary Discriminations." *NCF* 15 (1977): 30–45.

Thomson, James. *The Complete Poetical Works*. Ed. J. Logie Robertson. London: Oxford Univ. Press, 1951.

Thorpe, James, ed. *Relations of Literary Study*. New York: MLA, 1967.

Tillotson, Kathleen. *Novels of the 1840's*. Oxford: Oxford Univ. Press, 1954.

Torgovnick, Marianna. *The Visual Arts, Pictorialism, and the Novel: James, Lawrence, and Woolf*. Princeton: Princeton Univ. Press, 1985.

Tuveson, Ernest Lee. *The Imagination as a Means of Grace: Locke and the Aesthetics of Romanticism*. Berkeley: Univ. of Calif. Press, 1960.

Uspensky, Boris. *A Poetics of Composition: The Structure of the Artistic Text and Typology of a Compositional Form*. Trans. Valentina Zavarin and Susan Wittig. Berkeley: Univ. of Calif. Press, 1973.

Van Ghent, Dorothy. *The English Novel: Form and Function*. New York: Rinehart, 1953.

Varma, Devendra P. *The Gothic Flame*. London: Arthur Baker, and Morrison and Gibb, 1957.

Warren, Alba. *English Poetic Theory: 1825–1865*. Princeton: Princeton Univ. Press, 1950.

Watkinson, Raymond. *Pre-Raphaelite Art and Design*. Greenwich: New York Graphic Society, 1970.

Watson, J. R. *Picturesque Landscape and English Romantic Poetry*. London: Hutchinson Educational, 1970.

Watt, Ian. *The Rise of the Novel*. Berkeley: Univ. of Calif. Press, 1965.

————, ed. *The Victorian Novel: Modern Essays in Criticism*. New York: Oxford Univ. Press, 1971.

Welch, James D. "Tennyson's Landscapes of Time and a Reading of 'The Kraken.'" *VP* 14: 3 (Autumn 1976): 197–204.

Wellek, René and Austen Warren. *Theory of Literature*. New York: Harcourt Brace, 1956.

Welsh, Alexander. *The City of Dickens*. Oxford: Oxford Univ. Press, 1971.

Wendorf, Richard, ed. *Articulate Images: The Sister Arts from Hogarth to Tennyson*. Minneapolis: Univ. of Minnesota Press, 1983.

Williams, Raymond. *The Country and the City*. New York: Oxford Univ. Press, 1973.

————. *Culture and Society: 1780–1950*. New York: Harper & Row, 1958.

Wilson, Edmund. "Dickens: The Two Scrooges." *The Wound and the Bow*. Cambridge: Harvard Univ. Press, 1941: 1–104.

Wimsatt, W. K., Jr. *The Verbal Icon: Studies in the Meaning of Poetry*. Lexington: Univ. Press of Kentucky, 1962.

Woodring, Carl. "Nature and Art in the Nineteenth Century." *PMLA* 92 (1976): 193–202.

Woolf, Virginia. *The Waves*. New York: Harcourt Brace, 1923, 1959.

Wordsworth, William. *The Poetical Works of William Wordsworth*. Ed. Ernest de Selincourt. Vol. 2. Oxford: Clarendon Press, 1944.

————. *The Prelude or Growth of a Poet's Mind*. Ed. Ernest de Selincourt. Oxford: Clarendon Press, 1926.

Index